THE
HALL

Celebrating Hockey's Heritage, Heroes and Home

Kevin Shea ✳ Forewords by Lanny McDonald and Jeff Denomme

The National Treasure Series is a multi-book collection that focuses on the history, Honoured Members, artifacts and activities of the Hockey Hall of Fame in Toronto. The series tells the story of The Hall from its founding to its status as national icon, and features dramatic and compelling imagery from its unrivalled hockey photo collection.

CURRENT BOOKS IN THE NATIONAL TREASURE SERIES

A Century of NHL Memories - Rare Photos from the Hockey Hall of Fame (Fall 2017)

The Hall - Celebrating Hockey's Heritage, Heroes and Home (Fall 2018)

Conceived, designed and presented by Griffintown Media Inc.

nationaltreasureseries.com

NATIONAL TREASURE
SERIES

The Hall - Celebrating Hockey's Heritage, Heroes and Home
Kevin Shea

CONTENT CURATION
Griffintown Media in Partnership with the Hockey Hall of Fame

Published in Canada by Griffintown Media Inc.
5548 Saint-Patrick Street, Montreal, QC H4E 1A9
(514) 934-2474 | info@griffintown.com | griffintown.com

All photos were provided from the collections of the Hockey Hall of Fame

ISBN 978-0-9958630-3-3

Printed in Canada by Friesens | Manitoba

PRODUCTION CREDITS

CONTENT CURATION
Hockey Hall of Fame
Phil Pritchard
Craig Campbell
Steve Poirier
Kevin Shea

Griffintown Media Inc.
Salma Belhaffaf
Jim McRae

CONCEPT, DESIGN & PRODUCTION
Griffintown Media Inc.
Jim McRae, President
Salma Belhaffaf, Senior Designer
Katrysha Gellis, Project Coordinator
Jim Hynes, Assistant Editor
Judy Yelon, Proofreader

NATIONAL TREASURE
SERIES

...the magnificently restored bank building located at the corner of Yonge and Front Streets will be transformed as a cathedral to the icons of hockey, and the new Hall will be founded on the principles of Entertainment, Education and Excellence.

SCOTTY MORRISON
Report to City of Toronto Land Use Committee | December 1987

TABLE OF CONTENTS

FOREWORDS

Our family farm in Craigmyle, Alberta, had a pond where I took my first strides on skates at the age of five. A couple of years later, Mom and Dad would drive me to Hanna, 22 miles away, twice a week, to play hockey. It was fun to be following in the footsteps of both my dad and older brother, Lynn, and a great way to grow up.

I watched 'Hockey Night in Canada' every Saturday with my dad and brother. My sisters Donna and Dixie weren't that interested, but Dad, Lynn and I never missed a game. We cheered for the Toronto Maple Leafs. In fact, my dad was such a fan that my middle name is 'King,' after King Clancy.

Like every kid my age, I dreamed that someday I might make it to the NHL. I had a good junior career but no one, and I mean no one, was more excited than me to be drafted into the NHL in 1973. And imagine: I was selected by the Maple Leafs!

One of my former teammates, Mike Eaves, summed up the career of a hockey player. He said that you come into the league and try to find your place. Then, after a few years, you've found that place, you've established your spot and you finally belong. And just when you're feeling comfortable about belonging, it's all over. And it's true: you really can't believe how fast your career goes. Still, my playing career was a dream come true. I went out on top, carrying the Stanley Cup around the rink with the Calgary Flames in my final game. After 16 seasons in the NHL, what a great way to go!

If my NHL career was the realization of a dream, I can truthfully tell you that I never dreamed that in 1992 I would be inducted into the Hockey Hall of Fame.

I never wanted to imagine what life would be without hockey. Although I have a number of outside business interests, I was honoured to be offered a management position with the Calgary Flames on my retirement, and later played a key role with Hockey Canada.

One of the great delights of my professional life has been my involvement with The Hall. I joined the Selection Committee in June 2007. Being part of the process to elect Honoured Members has been an immense privilege.

In November 2014, my friend Pat Quinn passed away. He had been a player, coach and general manager, but most recently, had been chairman of The Hall. I was asked if I might be interested in the position. What an honour it was when The Hall's vice-chair, Jim Gregory, announced, "As a perennial supporter since his induction in 1992 and a member of the Selection Committee for the past nine years, Lanny is familiar with the affairs of the Hockey Hall of Fame just as the hockey world remembers his achievements during his outstanding playing career. While Lanny is highly recognized as an exceptional hockey player, he is also a dedicated family man, community benefactor, philanthropist and successful businessman whose leadership qualities will be a valuable asset to The Hall and its continued growth and development."

It was a very humbling day for me. It is a thrill and an honour to follow in the legacy created by those who came before me, guys like Bill Hay, Pat Quinn and Scotty Morrison. I take the responsibility very seriously and I truly appreciate the ongoing support from members of the board, Selection Committee and the outstanding team of management and staff.

As a kid who struggled around the frozen ponds of Alberta all those years ago dreaming of a career in hockey I have been blessed far beyond my wildest dreams. And I take none of it for granted. Deep down, I'm still that little kid, passionate about the game of hockey. The only thing different is, of course, the mustache!

Lanny McDonald, Chairman of the Board
HOCKEY HALL OF FAME

Growing up across the street from the Memorial Arena in Goderich, Ontario, I was typical of many Canadian kids: my winter revolved around hockey. My hometown, the salt mining capital of the world, also holds a distinguished place in hockey history as host of the Young Canada Week (YCW) pee-wee tournament since 1950. As an eight-year-old regular in the "old barn" I was thrilled to see 12-year-old Wayne Gretzky score his 100th and 101st goals of the 1972-73 season for Brantford in a 5-0 YCW win over Port Huron, Michigan.

In my first year on skates playing Tyke house league, I somehow earned the nickname 'Geraldine Jones' (after the fictional TV character played by comedian Flip Wilson). "When you're hot, you're hot; when you're not, you're not!" and "What you see is what you get!" were among "her" sayings that became popular catchphrases at the time. That year, I scored 0 goals, assisted on 0 goals (probably a minus 100) and I may have touched the puck once or twice all season. Things got much better the next year when I decided to follow in my dad's footsteps by trading shin guards for goalie pads, launching a somewhat successful travelling minor hockey career "between the pipes." Even though the 'Geraldine' moniker was short-lived, there was still something that rang true with the "hot or not" catchphrase, hence the pretext for my lack of success beyond the Junior 'C' level with the Clinton Mustangs...

So as "most hockey dreams die" (*see page 125 for context*), and after working at the local abattoir and grain elevators to help pay my way through college, I turned to the business side of sports. I remember reading a newspaper article in my first year of the Sports Administration Program at Durham College about the Hockey Hall of Fame's pending search for a new home led by respected longtime NHL referee-in-chief, Scotty Morrison. I thought, *what a cool opportunity that could be*, but sensed the timing was off since I was just starting college. Little did I know that a few years later I would mentor under Scotty starting with an internship in a pilot program offered to a select few sports admin grads.

My primary role as an intern was to provide logistical support in "moving The Hall" to Quebec City for a temporary exhibition as part of the 'Rendez-vous '87' festivities, coinciding with the famous winter carnival, featuring two games between NHL All-Stars and the Soviet Union National Team. As it turned out, the timing couldn't have been better for my employment prospects as Scotty's transition to The Hall portfolio was about to kick into high gear and I became his first full-time hire in April 1987 on the heels of the successful Rendez-vous project.

As I think about that newspaper article and the fortuitous events that brought me to this time in The Hall's history, I look back at the many highlights over the years growing with the organization. While playing an active role in the relocation and expansion from the CNE Grounds to BCE Place in the early 1990s was an immense undertaking in and of itself, the further expansion and revitalization of hockey's iconic destination attraction has been equally, if not more, challenging and rewarding.

Having flourished in downtown Toronto for 25 years, The Hall is a multi-faceted, not-for-profit organization and registered charity that celebrates and preserves the game, with 90,000 square feet of real estate and an extended reach far beyond its premises. It's a constantly evolving museum and place of entertainment; it's an archive, research and educational facility housing a vast collection of anything to do with hockey; it runs retail merchandising and hospitality businesses; it develops and fosters partnerships through the licensing of its intellectual property rights, exhibitions and other outreach services; it travels the world as custodian of hockey's most coveted prize, the Stanley Cup; and each year it organizes and presents a high-profile gala celebration honouring excellence and greatness in hockey.

I'm proud of The Hall's success in these pursuits and the people who make them happen. Mostly, I'm proud of what The Hall has become for hockey fans everywhere, whether in Goderich or around the globe.

Jeff Denomme, President & CEO
HOCKEY HALL OF FAME

HOCKEY HALL of FAME
LE TEMPLE de LA RENOMMÉE du HOCKEY

The Hockey Hall of Fame was founded in 1943 to establish a memorial to those who have developed Canada's great winter sport - ice hockey. Its mandate is to recognize and honour the achievements of individuals and teams who have brought special distinction to the game of hockey and those who have made a major contribution to the development and advancement of hockey anywhere in the world. Built in 1885, the historic bank building at BCE Place, Toronto began a new era as "a cathedral for the icons of hockey" officially opened to the public on June 18, 1993.

Le Temple de la renommée du hockey a été fondé en 1943 afin de commémorer les personnes qui ont aidé à développer le grand sport d'hiver du Canada - le hockey sur glace. Son principal but est de reconnaître et d'honorer les réalisations d'individus et d'équipes qui ont apporté une contribution

Most people think of the Hockey Hall of Fame, as a famous destination, and it's no wonder. Its iconic building, priceless trophies and artifacts, and hallowed membership have helped to make it both a national treasure and an international beacon, an irresistible draw for any hockey fan. It's even greater than that.

More than a static monument welcoming visitors to its doors, The Hall is on a journey of its own, reaching out from its famous corner on Toronto's Yonge and Front to the four corners of the hockey world, sharing the rich story of the game and also seeking to write its next chapter. From its founding in 1943 and particularly since its move downtown in '93, The Hall has been active in its outreach, supporting groups and causes with the same sense of fair play as the game it represents. It regularly visits with First Nations communities from coast to coast to coast and troops overseas, and welcomes women as Honoured Members alongside men. There is no separate category.

Over the years, The Hall has grown in public stature thanks in large part to the popularity of its ever-evolving exhibits and the stunning beauty of its historic home. It also enjoys dual citizenship, of sorts, being both proudly Canadian, reflecting the birthplace of hockey, and a "citizen" of the world, celebrating the common bonds of the game wherever it is played. In its partnership with the International Ice Hockey Federation (IIHF), The Hall attends major competitions from the World Championship to the Olympics and has dedicated the largest exhibit space in its museum to chronicle hockey's global reach.

Of course, The Hall is also closely aligned with the National Hockey League (NHL). It gloriously showcases the league's history from its beginning, safeguards its trophies — including the most famous one in all of professional sports — and honours its heroes. It tells the NHL story so well, in fact, that many people believe The Hall is owned and controlled by the league. It's not. Instead, it has grown from having full financial support from the league at its founding, to independent, not-for-profit status today.

Behind the scenes, The Hall has amassed the world's largest and most important hockey collection, including archives, resource materials, photos and artifacts, all carefully catalogued and stored at its Resource Centre. It's a treasure trove of information selflessly shared with students of the game worldwide.

The real appeal of The Hall, however, might be its magic. It can instantly transport hockey's greatest heroes back to their childhood and make children dream of becoming the game's next star. Virtually every visitor who passes through its doors is brought back to a time, place or memory personal to them. Few places in the world have that kind of power. Then again, there are few places in the world quite like the Hockey Hall of Fame.

THE BIRTH OF THE HALL

A Shoe Salesman's Vision for a Shrine

The history of the Hockey Hall of Fame always circles back to Captain James Thomas Sutherland, a Kingston, Ontario, shoemaker whose real passion was hockey.

Sutherland was born October 10, 1870. His family operated a boot-making business at the foot of Princess Street in Kingston. As a youngster, James watched hockey being played on the frozen Confederation Basin near the mouth of the Cataraqui River. Many of those playing in those shinny games were soldiers stationed at Fort Henry. Retired members of the British military often shared stories of the city's earliest games with the wide-eyed Sutherland.

Sutherland learned to play hockey in the same spot as the soldiers and became quite adept at the game. In fact, he played with the Athletic Club of Kingston in what many believe to be the first recognized hockey league. In 1910, he turned to coaching, helping organize the Kingston Frontenacs, who won the J. Ross Robertson Cup as OHA Junior champions in 1910 and 1911. During that time, Sutherland was also the district represent-ative for the Ontario Hockey Association (OHA), and by 1915, he was named president, serving in that capacity until 1918.

In December 1914, Sutherland was one of 21 delegates from across Canada to gather in Ottawa with the intent of forming a national organization that would oversee amateur hockey. Dr. W. F. Taylor was named the inaugural president of the Canadian Amateur Hockey Association (CAHA), and two years later, Sutherland was appointed to that position. He was so influential that in 1934, the Sutherland Cup, emblematic of the Junior 'B' Championship, was named after him. Today, following reorganization, the trophy is awarded to the winner of the Greater Ontario Junior Hockey League.

When the Great War beckoned, the 146th Battalion, Canadian Expeditionary Force, based in Kingston, began recruiting, and in 1915, Sutherland enlisted, rising to the rank of captain. While serving overseas, Captain Sutherland suggested the idea of presenting a trophy to the best junior hockey team in Canada to honour the young men who died in service. The idea was borne from the loss of two hockey-playing friends from his hometown, 'Scotty' Davidson and George Richardson, who were killed in the European conflict. "Past-president Capt. J.T. Sutherland spoke of the splendid work done by Canadian boys in France and suggested the erection of a suitable memorial to hockey players who have fallen," wrote the *Toronto Globe* on December 9, 1918. The idea garnered great enthusiasm, and soon afterwards, the Memorial Cup was introduced.

Sutherland was one of the first hockey historians, as knowledgeable in the history of the game as he was of current happenings, so when the Baseball Hall of Fame was estab-lished in 1936, he latched on to the idea and began lobbying for a similar institution for hockey, which he began championing in 1937, stating that such an institution should "(perpetuate) the memories of the men who have done so much to develop nationally and internationally, Canada's great winter sport." By December 1940, Baz O'Meara of the *Montreal Daily Star* climbed aboard the bandwagon, listing a parade of hockey stars from that era, and adding, "They've marched and are marching into the mythical hall of fame, even though we won't recognize it until Time drapes a halo around their glamourous feats until they've acquired the aura of antiquity."

The Royal Military College hockey program was initiated in Kingston in 1886. Here, the RMC Cadets of 1919 prepare for practice on an outdoor rink.

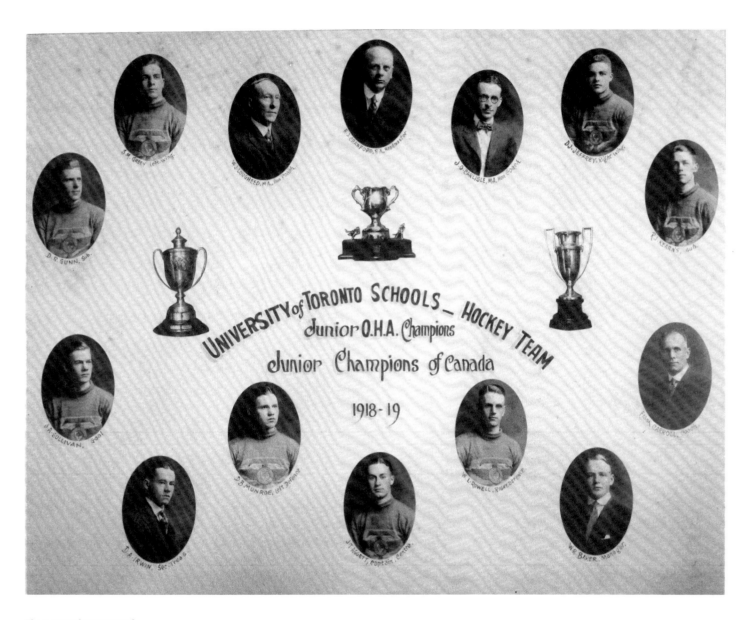

The inaugural recipients of the Memorial Cup as junior champions of Canada were the University of Toronto Schools, who won the trophy in 1919.

Sutherland suggested that the Hockey Hall of Fame should reside in the city where hockey was first established: Kingston. Using the argument that baseball's hall of fame was located in Cooperstown, the town in which that game was founded (it has long since been debunked as myth), Sutherland confidently argued that the first actual game of hockey was played in Kingston. "Historians are said to differ considerably on the place in which the great Caesar first saw the 'light of day,' and similarly in respect to the birthplace of Canada's national winter sport, hockey," stated Sutherland. "There may be some who still claim sundry and diverse places as being the authentic spot or locality. Whatever measure of merit the claim of other places may have, I think it is generally admitted and has been substantially proven on many former occasions that the actual birthplace of organized hockey is the city of Kingston, in the year 1888."

Although Sutherland had misstated the year (it was 1886), he based his claim on a game played between Queen's University and the Royal Military College at Dix's Rink, on the Confederation Basin in front of Kingston's municipal buildings. "The Royal Canadian Rifles at Tete-du-Pont barracks away back in the (18)60s formed the advanced guard for what has become Canada's great national game."

Sutherland's passion for Kingston as the birthplace of hockey was infectious, and journalists repeated his claim time and time again. William A. Hewitt, writing in the Toronto Maple Leafs program in 1937: "The Limestone City (Kingston) has generally been regarded in Canada as the birthplace of hockey because of the long and sustained interest in the sport and the marvelous enthusiasm (Sutherland) had exhibited through the years."

Both Montreal and Halifax also claimed that their city was the true birthplace of hockey, and that the Hockey Hall of Fame should be located in their city. The Montreal claim was based largely on a *Montreal Gazette* story: "The very game of hockey in fact had its beginnings at McGill (University). Hockey was played there in the early (18)70s and two McGill graduates drew up the first rules." A corroborative January 18, 1879 report in the *McGill University Gazette* reported that hockey had been played in Montreal "for more than three years."

Halifax countered with text isolated from John Regan's 1936 publication, *First Things in Acadia*: "It is a fact that for years, 1860 to 1890 and after, thousands of pairs of skates and hundreds of bundles of Indian-made hockey sticks were regularly shipped from Dartmouth and Halifax, Nova Scotia, and Saint John,

The Memorial Cup honours those who died in battle, including *(top)* George Richardson (France, 1916) and *(bottom)* Allan 'Scotty' Davidson (Belgium, 1915).

It was the vision of Kingston, Ontario, native Captain James T. Sutherland that led to the creation of the Hockey Hall of Fame in 1943.

New Brunswick, to sporting goods houses in New England, Montreal and Toronto for local distribution. Hockey or hurley did not start in the Maritimes at Confederation but long before."

Sutherland, commenting on Halifax's claim in the March 17, 1943 edition of the *Toronto Daily Star*, argued, "Kingston has at least an equal claim as Halifax to recognition as the birthplace of hockey."

On April 17, 1941, the CAHA formed a committee to determine the origins of hockey comprised of W.A. Hewitt, the Toronto-based journalist and secretary of the OHA (and father of broadcaster Foster Hewitt), George Slater, a Montreal hockey official, and Captain Sutherland, a lifetime member of the CAHA.

"Hockey needs its hall of fame because that is the only way the hardy pioneers of hockey can be given the honour that is their due," wrote the *Montreal Gazette* in 1941. "Without a hall, the feats of the oldsters and the rest will soon be forgotten." The paper added, "That's the task facing (the committee). It's a tough one, but they can do it." The committee set out to review cases presented by all three locations. Toronto wasn't considered at the time. As the CAHA reported, "Toronto came into hockey late, and while many good advocates up there could muster some notable reasons for its selection, it would undoubtedly be ruled out on the grounds that while its claims might be appealing, Montreal, Kingston, or even Ottawa, have more substance in their demands."

The Second World War was raging in Europe while the concept of a hockey hall of fame was being discussed. While most applauded the idea, not everyone was in favour. "War-time does not seem a propitious moment for starting it," wrote Charles Edwards in the March 9, 1943 edition of the *Calgary Herald*. NHL President Red Dutton, musing over the loss of life and scarce resources, also wondered about the timing, expressing his view in the April 29, 1943 edition of the *Winnipeg Evening Tribune* that it

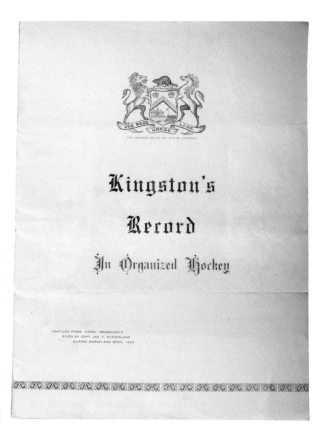

As the governing bodies of professional and amateur hockey, the National Hockey League and the Canadian Amateur Hockey Association appointed a committee to decide where hockey originated in order to award that city with the opportunity to house the Hockey Hall of Fame.

LEGEND OF THE HALL

The concept of honouring the greats goes back to Norse mythology, where the god Odin selected half of those who valiantly died in battle to travel to a majestic hall called *Valhalla* (from Old Norse for 'hall of the slain'). Inspired by this enduring legend, and following his accession to the throne of Bavaria in 1825, Crown Prince Ludwig erected grand monuments to honour "politicians, sovereigns, scientists and artists of the German tongue," calling it *Walhalla*. When it was completed, there were 96 busts as well as plaques for another 64 persons or events.

Inspired by Walhalla, Dr. Henry Mitchell McCracken, the Chancellor of New York University from 1891 to 1910, conceived the first hall of fame in North America. The Hall of Great Americans was created to honour prominent Americans who had greatly impacted U.S. history. McCracken established a template since employed by all halls of fame, insisting that he wanted to enshrine people who were not simply memorable, but truly famous. He established a board of electors comprised of people "of great character and sound judgement." The hall opened in New York in 1900. Its first 28 honourees included presidents, inventors and writers.

The movement to create other halls of fame accelerated in the 1930s. Stephen Carlton Clark, proprietor of a hotel in Cooperstown, New York, realized that an attraction like a hall of fame would draw tourists to his town, which had suffered economically because of the Great Depression. His lobbying for a baseball hall of fame, embracing the country's national sport, found traction, and on June 12, 1939, Judge Kenesaw Mountain Landis, commissioner of Major League Baseball, stood before 15,000 attendees and announced the opening of the National Museum and the Baseball Hall of Fame.

Such a momentous event prompted activity among hockey people, and the eventual founding of the Hockey Hall of Fame in 1943.

GROWING PAINS

A Tale of Two Cities

The idea for the Hockey Hall of Fame may have been conceived in Kingston, but, for reasons financial, another royal city up the lake would ultimately lay claim to the future hockey treasure.

Led by Captain James T. Sutherland, Mayor Harry Stewart and city councillors, plans moved forward to raise the money to build an institution worthy of hockey's illustrious history. It was decided that funding would come from a combination of sources, namely the NHL and CAHA, a municipal contribution, and a series of exhibition games featuring NHL stars.

While devoting countless hours to fundraising, Sutherland also amassed an excellent collection of photographs, sweaters, sticks and pucks that would populate The Hall once built.

William A. Hewitt, already the registrar/treasurer of the CAHA and secretary of the OHA, was named chairman and secretary to the board of directors of The Hall. The rest of the board was comprised of Abbie Coo (managing editor of the *Winnipeg Free Press* and president of the Manitoba Amateur Hockey Association), Mervyn 'Red' Dutton (president of the NHL), J.P. Fitzgerald (sports editor, *Toronto Telegram*), Wes McKnight (sports director of CFRB Radio in Toronto and host of the 'Hot Stove League' on 'Hockey Night in Canada' radio

broadcasts), Baz O'Meara (hockey columnist for the *Montreal Daily Star*), Lester Patrick (general manager of the New York Rangers and vice-president of Madison Square Garden), Art Ross (general manager of the Boston Bruins), and Frank Sargent (president of the CAHA).

As the City of Kingston began to raise the money to build an actual hall (officially registered as the International Hockey Hall of Fame), the governing committee began its task of electing the inaugural class of what would eventually be named Honoured Members. The board of directors, pleased with the players they had selected, later decided to add persons who had contributed greatly to the growth of the game without actually having played. The board added Lord Stanley of Preston, donor of the Stanley Cup, and Sir Montagu Allan, donor of the Allan Cup, calling them Builders.

The names and a short biography of each of the 11 initial honourees were entered in the Roll of Honour, a large book with black seal-skin covering and the title *International Hockey Hall of Fame* printed in ornate gold letters on the cover. The book was kept in the city treasurer's vault in Kingston pending the erection of the building.

Conn Smythe *(centre)* oversees construction as work begins on The Hall building at the CNE.

There was no induction gala at that time. Instead, Honoured Members were presented with a scroll that included their hockey biography. It wasn't always easy or timely. For example, Frank Nighbor was added to The Hall in 1947 but wasn't presented with his scroll until November 14, 1951. President James Garvin made the presentation during periods of an exhibition game between the NHL's Montreal Canadiens and the Pembroke Lumber Kings of the Eastern Canada Senior Hockey League, with proceeds given to The Hall.

As the city continued its fundraising, several exhibition games were played with proceeds contributing to the money needed for The Hall. On February 24, 1947, the NHL's Boston Bruins faced the OHA Senior Hamilton Tigers. In another game on October 15, 1947, the Stanley Cup champion Toronto Maple Leafs faced the Allan Cup champion Montreal Royals.

Kingston, however, struggled to raise money. It seemed that every time they got close to their target, the price jumped. Despite a running tally exceeding $45,000, just shy of the original estimate of $50,000 for construction, the cost of labour and building materials continued to skyrocket, and by 1947, a new target of $150,000 was set. By 1954, the price tag had catapulted to $250,000. Dreams were quickly fading. In June 1955, Captain Sutherland realized the futility of his pursuit and admitted that the City of Kingston was not able to build The Hall.

"Captain Sutherland was quite upset; distressed, in fact," recalls historian Bill Fitsell. Momentum slowed even further when the 'Father of Hockey in Kingston' passed away on September 30, 1955, just shy of his 85th birthday, his dream unfulfilled. His gravestone was engraved with the logo of his beloved but unbuilt hall of fame. Nine days after Sutherland's death, his widow, Ethel, also died. To make matters even more dire, Mayor Stuart Crawford also passed away shortly thereafter. "He was the other main link in terms of organizing the hall of fame," continues Fitsell, "so when Sutherland and Crawford died, all the impetus for the Kingston location for the hall also died."

Although Kingston had worked so diligently for so long to create The Hall, the NHL and CAHA had grown impatient. Frank Selke, general manager of the Montreal Canadiens,

William A. Hewitt served as the first chairman of the Hockey Hall of Fame. He was inducted as a Builder in 1947.

FIRST CLASS

On May 1, 1945, W.A. Hewitt announced the first Honoured Members for induction to the Hall of Fame, a who's who of hockey all-stars to that point in time.

Hobey Baker | first American hockey star

Charlie Gardiner | outstanding goalie with Chicago

Eddie Gerard | three Stanley Cup championships Ottawa Senators (2), Toronto St. Patricks (1)

Frank McGee | once scored 14 goals in a Stanley Cup playoff game

Howie Morenz | one of the most dominant players of the 1920s and twice the NHL's scoring leader

Tom Phillips | excellent two-way player who twice won the Stanley Cup

Harvey Pulford | captain of the four-time Stanley Cup champion Ottawa Silver Seven

Hod Stuart | one of the first professional hockey players to compete for the Stanley Cup

Georges Vézina | allowed the fewest goals in seven seasons; four times in the NHA, three times in the NHL

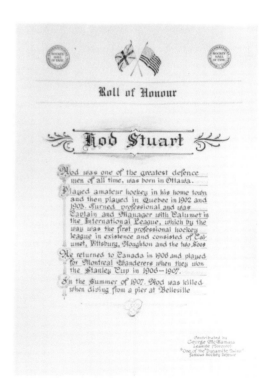

Inductees to The Hall received their Roll of Honour, such as the one prepared for Hod Stuart, a member of the inaugural class.

pleaded with the team owners to consider a new location. "I feared that if we didn't do so in our time, The Hall would never be built."

NHL President Clarence Campbell agreed, and the team owners suggested that Selke form a committee to try to revive interest in building The Hall in Kingston, but after a few inquiries, the idea was stillborn. Dink Carroll of the *Montreal Gazette*, wrote, "Now that the Hockey Hall of Fame has fallen flat on its face from neglect in Kingston, mightn't it be a good idea to transfer it to Montreal, which has a more valid claim as the original site of organized hockey than the Ontario city?"

Toronto Maple Leafs owner Conn Smythe suggested that few fans would have visited Kingston and suggested the thriving metropolis of Toronto with its much larger population base as a more appropriate home for The Hall.

Although hockey's earliest roots point to locations like Halifax, Windsor (Nova Scotia) and Montreal, Toronto turned out to be a logical spot for The Hall due to its location. In fact, there was a precedent: In 1947, Harry Price, the chairman of the Sports Committee for the Canadian National Exhibition (CNE), and his colleague, Bert Powell, took action enlisting support for the construction of a museum dedicated to Canadian athletes.

The CNE Grounds were a perfect location for a sports museum. Located on the periphery of downtown Toronto, the CNE had been founded in 1879 as the Toronto Industrial Exhibition and had since become Canada's largest community event. Taking place for 18 days leading up to and including Labour Day, the CNE is one of this country's great traditions, and attracts approximately 1.5 million visitors each year.

"Unlike many others who had talked but had gone no further, Mr. Price and Mr. Powell set the machinery in motion," states the 1962 souvenir program from Canada's Sports Hall of Fame. "Mr. Powell made a cross-country tour of Canada and in many centres, discussed the plan and found in all cases, it met with unanimous approval."

A billboard on the grounds of the CNE in Toronto announces the upcoming arrival of The Hall.

Facing Page

TOP. An architect's rendering of The Hall comes to life.

BOTTOM. The site under construction.

ROOFTOP PROPOSAL BY NEON PRODUCTS OF CANADA LIMITED

Frank Selke donated a collection of sticks used by players to score their 200th NHL goal.

The CNE's Price made certain that a prime location was provided for the building that would house Canada's Sports Hall of Fame. George Bell, the Toronto Parks Commissioner, offered "the most desirable location of all – right in the centre of the park."

It took eight years, but on August 24, 1955, Canada's Sports Hall of Fame opened to much acclaim, holding its opening ceremonies in a building on the CNE Grounds that had once housed the Stanley Barracks, ironically, named after Lord Stanley of Preston, who donated hockey's magnificent trophy. Although their inaugural class of inductees included two hockey players (Howie Morenz as well as multi-sport athlete Lionel Conacher), they did not subsequently induct hockey players because of the plans for the hockey hall at Kingston. In fact, Canada's Sports Hall of Fame had purposely not included hockey in its exhibits so as not to invade Kingston's territory.

Meanwhile, the NHL owners met in Palm Beach, Florida, during the winter of 1957 and among the topics discussed was the fate of a hall of fame. On February 5, the NHL reported that it would install a year-round hockey shrine at the CNE. "All NHL clubs are giving full support," stated Frank Selke, who committed to contributing his collection of hockey sticks used by players to score their 200th NHL goal. The sticks had been most recently displayed at the Montreal Forum.

Conn Smythe, who became the majority shareholder and president of Maple Leaf Gardens in 1947, was not only one of the most powerful persons in the NHL, but also, one of the most important individuals in the establishment of The Hall in Toronto. Smythe was chairman of the NHL owners' committee as well as a member of The Hall's board of directors. He used his platforms to lobby fellow owners into buying into his Toronto plan. Curiously, the other principal in the endeavour was Frank Selke, also a member of the board. Smythe was managing director of the Maple Leafs in April 1946 when Selke acrimoniously left Smythe's employ and three months later, joined the

archrival Montreal Canadiens as their general manager. Their strained relationship had grown appreciably warmer through their mutual work on behalf of The Hall.

Smythe and Selke found wonderful partners who agreed to assist in making The Hall a reality. One was James Norris Jr., owner of the Chicago Black Hawks. The other was Price, who had been named president of the CNE. He announced that one of his mandates was to build the permanent home for The Hall at the CNE. At a luncheon in Montreal on January 31, 1958, the death knell was finally sounded for Kingston. NHL President Campbell announced that The Hall was going to be built on the CNE Grounds, separate from Canada's Sports Hall of Fame.

While the Kingston organizing committee was crushed by the news, the dream did not die completely. The city continued Captain Sutherland's quest, and in 1962, the International Hockey Hall of Fame was created in Kingston, and three years afterwards, found a home in a new building on the grounds of

1. Red Dutton; 2. Lloyd Turner; 3. Frank Goheen; 4. Ching Johnson; 5. Aurel Joliat; 6. Frank Boucher; 7. Al Pickard; 8. Bill Cook; 9. George Hay; 10. Duke Keats; 11. Dit Clapper; 12. Eddie Shore; 13. Conn Smythe; 14. King Clancy; 15. Wm. Northey; 16. Frank Foyston; 17. George Dudley; 18. Frank Fredrickson; 19. Lester Patrick; 20. Newsy Lalonde; 21. Frank Nighbor; 22. Joe Malone; 23. Herb Gardiner; 24. W. A. Hewitt; 25. Hugh Lehman; 26. Art Ross; 27. Cyclone Taylor; 28. Dickie Boon; 29. Claude Robinson; 30. Moose Johnson; 31. Paddy Moran.

The Star Weekly MAGAZINE, December 12, 1959

To fuel interest in building The Hall, previously inducted Honoured Members attended a luncheon on September 5, 1959, which was designated as 'Hockey Day' at the CNE.

raised in the land of Canada's neighbour (four of the six NHL teams), but here it stands to honour the deeds of hockey players from both sides of the border."

Among the Honoured Members present were Frank Boucher, Bill Cook, Frank Foyston, Mickey Ion, Ching Johnson, Newsy Lalonde and Eddie Shore. They watched as the new inductees were welcomed into the ranks.

The ceremony ended with the raising of pennants from the six NHL teams on flagpoles situated in front of the building. Don McKenney did the honours for the Boston Bruins, Pierre Pilote for the Chicago Black Hawks, Sid Abel for the Detroit Red Wings, Jean Béliveau on behalf of the Montreal Canadiens, Doug Harvey for the New York Rangers and George Armstrong for the Toronto Maple Leafs.

The main hall was opened solely during the three weeks of the CNE, but an exception was made during Grey Cup Week that December when The Hall took advantage of the crowds at Exhibition Stadium and opened for two hours each weekday and also on game day. The Hall enjoyed outstanding attendance in its first year. Hewitson noted that the Stanley Cup was, by far, the item everyone had come to see.

The choice of Toronto as home for The Hall was proving to be wise.

Newly inducted Honoured Members received a crest of The Hall's logo.

FRONT & CITY CENTRE

Moving Downtown

THE BANK BUILD

The magnificent piece of architecture in Toronto's downtown core actually straddles Toronto's storied history. The fact that the Great Hall of the Hockey Hall of Fame even exists today is nothing short of miraculous, but there is quite a story about this beautiful and historic building.

By the middle of the 19th century, Toronto's growth had exploded. The exponential population growth can be attributed to Irish immigration resulting from the potato famine. The effects of the Great Famine also permanently altered Toronto. In 1847 alone, more than 38,000 Irish flooded into the city.

With the population explosion came the need for various services, including banks. And within the one block area that was bordered by Yonge, Wellington, Bay and Front (now encompassed by Brookfield Place), various banks sprung up at the turn of the 19th century. The Bank of Montreal was inaugurated in Montreal in 1818 and opened its first Toronto branch in a small building at Yonge and Front in 1845. When the bank's client base grew, space became cramped, and the bank sought to replace this building with one much larger and more august for the head office. The architectural firm of Darling and Curry was contracted in 1885 to design a suitable building on the same site.

Frank Darling, a Scarborough, Ontario native, and Samuel Curry, from nearby Port Hope, worked together between 1880 and 1891, designing several buildings, perhaps most notably, the Victoria Hospital for Sick Children in Toronto on College Street, now the headquarters of Canadian Blood Services. Darling, incidentally, was an avid hockey player and a member of the Toronto Hockey Club, one of the city's first teams.

When it was completed in 1886, the two-storey building was the largest in Canada. The exterior was constructed of sandstone that had been quarried near Cleveland, Ohio. Around the perimeter of the building were various carvings depicting arts and industry, created magnificently by Holbrook and Mollington. The entrance was positioned diagonally straddling the corners of both Yonge and Front, creating a striking visual effect.

Ornately designed in the Beaux-Arts style, the interior of the octagonal hall was the most opulent of its day, reflective of the prosperity enjoyed by Toronto at the time, and featured a sensational stained glass skylight, created by the Robert McCausland Company in French Renaissance style.

The west side of the building included an office for the bank manager, a boardroom and a private apartment, which was also used by the bank manager. The bank vault, now the permanent home of the original Stanley Cup donated by Lord Stanley of Preston, as well as the bands removed from the Stanley Cup, is the oldest bank vault in Canada. The building has been called "the most spirited, self-assured building erected in 19th-century Toronto." Christopher Hume, the architecture critic for the *Toronto Star*, noted that "it dates from an age of great prosperity and optimism." The Dictionary of Canadian Biography states that the firm of Darling and Curry "anticipated the taste for monumental public architecture that would sweep North America in the first decades of the twentieth century."

From its completion in 1886, the building served as the Bank of Montreal's head office until 1949, when they moved to a location at King and Bay, with the Yonge and Front location continuing as a branch until it was closed in 1982. The building, designated a Historical Property, sat largely unused until the latter part of that decade, when it was renovated and included in the development of BCE Place, now called Brookfield Place. As part of its agreement with the City of Toronto, BCE (Bell Canada Enterprises) was to restore the building to its original splendour and dedicate the space to a not-for-profit cultural institution. While several groups applied for the once-in-a-generation opportunity, the Hockey Hall of Fame was an ideal candidate, and both BCE and the City of Toronto agreed to the new tenants.

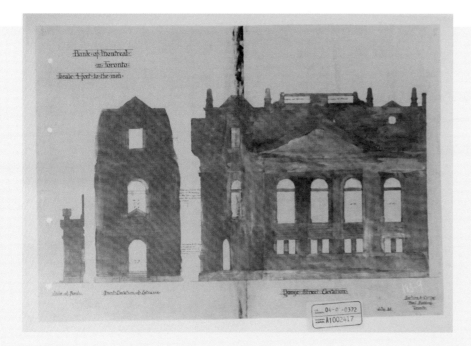

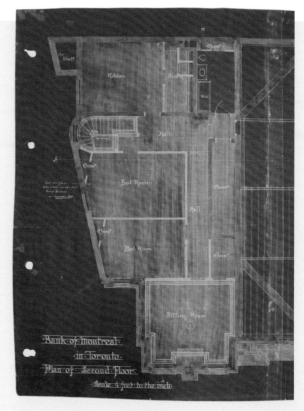

The Hall had 10,760 square feet at the CNE, although only half was used for the exhibits. Morrison suggested, "I'm thinking of 50,000 square feet in a building that would serve not only as a Hall of Fame, but also a hockey museum and entertainment centre. The days are gone when you could hang up a pair of old skates. You need interactivity and hands-on exhibits."

It wasn't long before he found what he was looking for. "Interested parties put us together with the Bell People (Bell Canada Enterprises, better known as BCE) and the solution they proposed was ideal."

As part of an agreement with the City of Toronto, the developer (BCE) hoped to build towers to get extra density in Toronto's downtown core. Under the Ontario Planning Act, the local city councillor had the authority to negotiate with BCE, allowing them extra density in exchange for certain subsidies that would benefit the ward. The trade-off was to make available the bank building at the corner of Front and Yonge Streets, with BCE required to restore the building to its original splendour, as well as offer an additional 40,000 square feet made available to a non-profit, cultural institution rent-free for a 99-year lease.

The Bank of Montreal had moved its head office to a much larger building at the corner of King and Bay Streets, just blocks away from the building at Yonge and Front, which remained a branch until it was closed in 1982. Since then, the building had sat largely unused for most of the decade, although at various times, discussions had involved turning the building into an art gallery, a museum of photography or the Canadian Business Hall of Fame. The Hockey Hall of Fame was an ideal candidate, and on July 12, 1988, both BCE and the City of Toronto agreed to the new tenants.

The result was highly exciting to those involved in The Hall's relocation. "We agreed that the location would provide unparalleled ease of recognition and accessibility, situated only a short walk from Union Station, Toronto's central commuter hub," stated NHL president Ziegler.

Scotty Morrison had looked for a space that was at least 50,000 square feet, and the new location perfectly fit the bill. The bank building was 15,000 square feet with an additional 35,000 square feet at concourse level.

Morrison laid out the principles for The Hall: "Entertainment, Education and Excellence." David Taylor had been hired from his role as general manager of the Corporation of Massey Hall and Roy Thomson Hall to oversee the construction of the building as president of The Hall. He commented, "There will be no better place in the world for fans to totally absorb themselves in the game they love. The new Hockey Hall of Fame will become an international focal point for hockey, celebrating Canada's gift to the world."

Signs announce the new location of The Hall, being readied for hockey fans in the former Bank of Montreal in downtown Toronto.

Morrison assured all that "The Hall will have the charisma that such a historic building deserves." The bank, even before renovations, was already stunning. "The Hall is an exuberant expression of architecture as decoration," stated Christopher Hume, the architecture critic for the *Toronto Star*. "With its rich paneling, dragon-motif frieze, painted lunettes, commemorative murals, Corinthian columns and Lincrusta walls, this is sheer bravura. Truly, this is a bank from the Golden Age of Banks."

Renovating the vacant bank was a monumental undertaking. Workers began the painstaking task of restoring the grandeur of the building by removing as many as 18 layers of paint that had accumulated for more than 100 years from the ornately decorated wood, most recently, a pale blue covered in dust and dirt. The team did a masterful job, transforming a 70-by-70-foot room into a showpiece that not only serves as the pre-eminent sports museum in the world, but a stunning attraction for the city, the province and the country. The original rococo architecture was kept largely intact, so much so that the Toronto firm of Holbrook and Mollington used the original drawings of architect Frank Darling to recreate the interior carvings on the west side of the Great Hall, framing the mezzanine in the process.

The Great Hall was described in some detail. "The huge arched windows of plate glass, extravagant for their time, signal the size of the interior. To the left of the south portico stands the massive stone figure of Hermes, who has carried the weight of the building's chimney on his shoulders for more than 100 years. Four tall piers support a pediment on each of the two main facades. Near the top of these piers, the lavish architectural detail continues with carved masks and sculpted shields. Below each of these masks are carved elements that symbolize the arts and industry. The most striking of the city's 19th-century bank buildings stands today as one of its most beautiful restorations. It confirms a commitment to architectural preservation on the part of the City of Toronto, and Brookfield Place."

Scotty Morrison, appointed the NHL's vice-president of project development for the Hockey Hall of Fame, led a committee that found the perfect new location for The Hall in Toronto's downtown core.

Scotty Morrison (*fifth from left*) is joined by Hall staff prior to the restoration of the historic bank building — the future new home for The Hall. This 1989 photo shows President and CEO Jeff Denomme (*far right*) and Vice-President, Resource Centre, and Curator Phil Pritchard (*second from right*).

A GLASS OF ITS OWN

Rising 45 feet above the floor of the Great Hall is an incredible stained-glass ceiling, sensationally colourful and wonderfully symbolic, that spans more than 40 feet across. It was created by Robert McCausland, a second-generation designer and manufacturer of stained-glass. Robert's father, Joseph, had moved to Upper Canada with his family in 1835, when he was seven, and in 1862, established Canada Stained Glass Works, one of this country's first such enterprises, in Toronto. By 1881, Robert McCausland partnered with his father in a firm now renamed Joseph McCausland and Son.

Places of worship were the mainstay of the company's business, but they had already earned a sterling reputation for their work. In 1886, they were awarded the contract to create the stained-glass dome at the Bank of Montreal in downtown Toronto.

The dome was adorned with mythological figures as well as eight sections; seven for the provinces in the Dominion at the time and one for Canada. The sections included a crown for British Columbia, a bison for Manitoba, maple leaves for Ontario, a lion for Quebec, a fish for Nova Scotia, a ship for New Brunswick, trees for Prince Edward Island plus a beaver to represent Canada. Alberta and Saskatchewan didn't enter Confederation until 1905 and Newfoundland and Labrador joined in 1949. The territories, Northwest Territories (1870), Yukon (1898) and Nunavut (1999), are not included.

The stained-glass panels of this building cemented Robert McCausland's already outstanding reputation. The *Toronto Star*'s descriptive prose paid tribute to the magnificence of the ceiling: "Twenty-four panels fan along the ribs of the window. Unsleeping dragons in jewel colours guard cornucopias of gold from marauding eagles. Above the dragons, the Dominion, as it was, is represented by the seven spherical emblems of the provinces, an eighth for the Canadian beaver, and, at the epicentre, a blazing sun."

THE GREAT FIRE

April 19, 1904, was a date that would live in infamy in Toronto. On a cold and blustery night, a fire started in a downtown building — likely caused by a stove left burning at the end of the day — and spread through the area, leaving devastation in its wake. Flames quickly engulfed businesses and within an hour, every firefighter in the city had been called in. Shortly before midnight, the inferno had reached Front Street, where it continued south to where Union Station now stands, and raced east toward Yonge.

The blaze raged through the night, fuelled by buildings constructed mostly of wood, the vast majority of which had no sprinkler systems. The fire was brought under control after nine hours, but not before it destroyed 104 buildings; miraculously, no one was killed. Damage was estimated at more than $10 million (approximately $270 million in today's currency), dealing a serious blow to the city's commerce. Five thousand people were left without work, many temporarily until their companies could be re-established.

The blaze levelled 30 acres of the downtown, including much of what is today's Brookfield Place. It was described by *The Globe* as "the most valuable business block in the city." The buildings on the Yonge Street side were spared, and the facades of 12 of the edifices have been restored and continue to occupy their original positions on Yonge and Wellington Streets.

The Bank of Montreal was one of the lucky ones to survive Toronto's Great Fire. A plaque on the exterior indicates that the building has since been designated a historic site under the Ontario Heritage Act. It is now The Hall's home.

The Great Hall is grand for so many reasons: the heritage architecture, the Stanley Cup which resides there, the NHL's merit trophies and the Honoured Members' plaques. Often overlooked is a skyward glance at the gasp-inspiring stained-glass dome that serves as a most extraordinary canopy over the most magnificent building in Toronto.

When The Hall began its plans to move into the space, there was a need to refresh and repair the stained-glass dome, which had weathered the storms of 105 years. The McCauslands firm had done extraordinary work in 1886, so the search didn't need to go far. Andrew McCausland, the great-grandson of Robert McCausland and president and CEO of Robert McCausland Ltd., was awarded the contract in 1991 and went immediately to work on this gargantuan task.

"Some of the glass panels were badly slumped and the glass was beginning to fall out of the lead," reported Andrew. The restoration involved photographing, numbering and meticulously wrapping each panel before gently removing them to be worked upon at the company's studios. Pattern paper was then placed over each individual panel and rubbed with carbon to replicate the pattern of the lead lines. Each of the panels was soaked and cleaned and the aging lead detached. The result was a massive puzzle of glass pieces, each carefully identified by its

location to facilitate the subsequent return to the ceiling once readied. The panels were then placed on the carbon-rubbed pattern paper to guide the shape so that new leading could be made. A waterproof cement was injected between the lead and the glass to maintain the dome's integrity against Toronto weather. Once completed, the panels were transported back to the future Hall, where scaffolding had been erected in order to reinstall the stained-glass panels.

The Historic Sites and Monuments Board of Canada has placed a plaque in the Great Hall to signify the beauty and historical significance of the stained-glass dome created (and refreshed) by the McCausland family's firm.

Hockey's Holy Grail, the original Stanley Cup bowl, is permanently housed in the Great Hall, and so are all of the merit trophies awarded annually by the NHL. The opulent room also contains the Honoured Member Walls, spotlighting the Players, Builders and Referees/Linesmen who have contributed to hockey so significantly that they have been elevated to this august status. The original vault, used to protect the bank's most valuable assets, still serves a similar purpose, now guarding the original Stanley Cup donated by Lord Stanley of Preston in 1893, as well as the silver bands no longer encircling the Cup but now flattened in order to display the teams and often the players who claimed the trophy over the years. The vault in the Great Hall is the oldest vault in Canada.

During the 19th century, when the bank was built, it was common practice to include an apartment for the manager. This area is on the western-most side of the Great Hall, and overlooks Front Street. On the second floor of the bank building, which faces the display area, are two board rooms. One is the upper vault while the other is the original board room, classically appointed in leather and oak.

While it is the showpiece, the Great Hall is just one facet of the shrine itself. Design Workshop, in collaboration with The Hall's staff and most notably its versatile and industrious creative director, Ray Paquet, was tasked with designing the rest of The Hall. "The trick was to come up with something that was a memorial to the game but that also appealed to people who aren't mad about hockey. It had to be fun and interesting." Taylor Manufacturing, creators of the exhibits, examined the plans and brought the history of hockey to life. The displays and interactive area, located on the concourse level, are fascinating, exciting complements to the Great Hall.

Restored and renovated, polished and preened, the Hall of Fame was ready for its June 18, 1993 opening at Yonge and Front Streets.

The original scale model for The Hall illustrated how the new space would be allocated for the 1993 opening.

A GRAND OPENING

The New Hall is Anointed

Renovations to the bank building were continuing, but the project had fallen far behind and there was great fear that The Hall would not be ready to open on the targeted date.

David Taylor had been hired to help oversee the move of The Hall from the CNE Grounds to downtown Toronto. While Taylor led the design, management and staff teams, a select group of employees who knew the collection, contributed significantly in weekly meetings to comment on aspects of the design and how best to populate The Hall with appropriate artifacts, photographs and captions to entertain and educate visitors. One of those who contributed was the current president and CEO, Jeff Denomme.

"I was Scotty Morrison's first hire when The Hall was at the CNE," explains Denomme. "Although initially my title was Special Projects Coordinator, whithin a few months The Hall's finances and IT platforms were added to my responsibilities. Scotty was my mentor and a great ambassador for The Hall. The timing was ideal. I was involved at the very beginning of the relocation process right through to completion."

As renovations were ongoing, Taylor got a call that threw the team into panic mode. Wesley Scott, the president of Bell, called and firmly stated, "We've had our money tied up in the development of the (Bell) Great Hall for some time, and I want you to know that we are upset by the delay. We are holding a golf tournament in Scarborough and we'd like to have a dinner for our participants afterwards in the Bell Great Hall."

Great idea. Bad timing.

"I gulped three times but I had to say yes," Taylor recalls. First off, the room was in the midst of construction. Secondly, The Hall staff had never previously executed events, but each staff member scurried about getting the site prepared and Bell had a wonderful dinner in the Great Hall after their golf tournament. "It shows how a group of great people could work together with a major surprise in the midst of the chaos of construction," says Taylor. "They made things happen for an important business partner."

There were other obstacles that needed to be hurdled that had nothing to do with construction. One was a lingering perception that it was the 'NHL Hall of Fame,' and there was bitterness towards the league at the time, particularly among former players concerning their pensions and the notion of missed opportunities in light of the emerging economics from the birth of salary disclosure. On April 1, 1992, the current players had voted overwhelmingly to strike after rejecting the owners' final offer on a new collective bargaining agreement (CBA) that involved free agency, arbitration, playoff bonuses, pensions and hockey card revenue. The strike ended on April 10, but while the players and the league agreed to a two-year deal retroactive to the start of the 1991-92 season, hard feelings remained.

Alan Tonks, chairman of the Municipality of Metropolitan Toronto *(right)*, presents a proclamation declaring the week of June 14 to 20, 1993 as Hockey Hall of Fame Week to Scotty Morrison *(left)* and David Taylor *(centre)*.

TOP. The Hall's downtown location was officially opened on June 18, 1993, by *(left to right)* Scotty Morrison, Governor General of Canada Ray Hnatyshyn and Hall President David Taylor.

BOTTOM. Scotty Morrison is interviewed by Sports Radio The Fan (now Sportsnet 590 The Fan) at The Hall's opening.

"I don't think the owners took the players seriously," said Bob Goodenow, president of the National Hockey League Players' Association. "It wasn't until the strike that they understood that the players were serious."

In addition, a number of the Honoured Members held the belief that The Hall did not carry the same prominence and scope as other sports halls of fame.

The Hall mandated that the new location would be so outstanding that Honoured Members would be immensely proud, their dignity honoured and the game's integrity intact while providing a terrific guest experience. So the launch of the new location had to be something quite grand, one that made a statement.

After some brainstorming, it was decided that all of the living Honoured Members and their wives would be brought into Toronto to participate in the grand opening of the new location. Despite the animosity towards the NHL that spilled over to The Hall, about 80 percent of invitees accepted an invitation.

On June 17, 1993 – the day before the public opening – Honoured Members from across North America arrived in Toronto, gathering at the Royal York Hotel for an opportunity to trade memories and a few laughs. Each was presented with a Hockey Hall of Fame blazer, ring and passes that they could sign and hand out to family, friends and fans. "We wanted to increase their sense of celebrity, which had been missing," suggested Taylor.

The group was given a tour of the new Hall, examining the displays and playing the interactive games. Leaf great Darryl Sittler was encouraged to test the Slap Shot exhibit and proceeded to destroy the goaltender target. Within a day, the exhibit was enhanced and replaced.

Prepared and polished, The Hall was officially opened on June 18, 1993.

After breakfast at the hotel, with thousands of hockey fans lining the route, the Honoured Members climbed into convertibles and were driven the 300 yards along Front Street to The Hall. At the traditionally busy corner of Yonge and Front Streets,

The Minnes family from Kingston, Ontario, was welcomed as the first guests through the turnstiles when The Hall opened at its new location.

GHOST IN THE HALL

The Hall is haunted!

That's the rumour that has been swirling around the city for decades, based on an actual event befitting a ghost story.

The apparition, apparently, is that of a young woman who worked in the building when it operated as the Bank of Montreal and who tragically took her own life at the start of work one winter's day.

Dorothea Mae Elliott, just 19, was described by co-workers as being "full of life and always smiling," "the life of the party" and "a beautiful girl" who resembled film star Rita Hayworth.

But something was troubling her.

On March 11, 1953, Elliott arrived at the bank before 8:00 am. "This was much earlier than she was expected to be in," explained Len Redwood, the bank's longtime messenger. Kidded by her co-workers at being in so early, Dorothea simply shrugged and smiled. Doreen Bracken, a co-worker, recalled Elliott wearing a blue knitted dress, looking "distressed and dishevelled."

Elliott went upstairs to the women's washroom, and seemed to stay there for some time. Redwood recounted that she came downstairs for a moment, and then returned to the second floor. A co-worker, Zeta Rushbrook, went upstairs just after 9:00 and rushed, screaming, to the balcony that overlooked the main floor of the bank. Redwood hurtled the stairs, only to discover Elliott's body slumped in a Windsor chair.

Elliott had quietly taken the bank's .38 calibre revolver, hidden in a drawer in case of incident, into the washroom, where she shot herself in the head. Redwood and an ambulance attendant carried her, mortally wounded, down the stairs to an ambulance. "We didn't hear a shot," remembered Bracken.

Elliott died of her wounds 22 hours later at St. Michael's Hospital. "Doctors were amazed she had lived so long," reported the *Toronto Daily Star*.

The *Toronto Telegram* reported that the "attractive young brunette may have been despondent over a love affair." *The Star* announced her death the next day, surmising that loneliness was the cause as her boyfriend had left Toronto "to take a job on the boats." Her co-workers knew the real story. They reported that Elliott was having an affair with the branch manager, a married man, who maintained an apartment on the second floor of the bank.

Since that date, strange occurrences have been reported with some regularity in the bank building. Lights flicking on, then off. Doors and windows opening and closing without anyone around. Faint sounds and echoes emanating from empty areas of the bank. "We all felt something like there was someone watching us, but you couldn't see them," Redwood recalled. The remaining female staff members refused to use the second-floor washroom, and the bank was forced to build one in the basement. The cleaning staff claimed they heard unusual noises after dark. It took some time, but eventually, the uneasiness settled down. "Sometimes I got kind of edgy, but most of the time I didn't worry about it," shrugged Redwood. "I guess you get kind of used to it."

One of the last employees of the Bank of Montreal to have worked in the building recalled that the ghost of Dorothea was prevalent all through her employment there. "In the mid-80s, (the building) was being used as general office space for the computer architecture group of the bank. Dorothea's antics were very real to the team that had their office cubicles on the main banking level. Imagine leaving your desk to go two cubicles over to use the copy machine and coming back to find your desk in disarray, your coffee spilled and your filing cabinets locked! Hardly a prank, as there were only three people in the building and none close enough to pull this off. Incidents like this occurred on a regular basis; less frequently during the day but with great regularity after 6:00pm."

When considering the bank building as the new location for The Hall, Scotty Morrison was apprised of the fact that many felt that the building was haunted by a ghost named Dorothea. "Somebody did ask me if I realized the place was haunted. That was early in negotiations and I never gave it a second thought."

Former Toronto Maple Leaf star Ron Ellis, now program director, HHOF Development Association, has frequently been told about Dorothea through the years. He just shrugs: "After playing for 'Punch' Imlach, nothing frightens me!"

And yet, the haunting spirit still seems to remind of her presence. Unusual occurrences like footsteps heard in the empty Great Hall, flickering lights, an eerie presence that can't be explained are all attributed to the ghost of The Hall — Dorothea Mae Elliott.

traffic had been blocked off. As each Honoured Member left his car, he was handed a hockey stick, and there, standing in a semi-circle in front of the bank building, and with the excited, cheering crowd looking on, participated in the world's largest faceoff to symbolically anoint the new Hockey Hall of Fame.

The Honoured Members themselves were among those offering rave reviews.

"In every player, there is a fan," stated Ken Dryden. "We looked up to the greats when we were kids."

"This is the best thing to happen to hockey in a hundred years," exclaimed Gump Worsley.

"I feel like a kid again," said Lanny McDonald, seeming to capture the sentiment of fellow Honoured Members with the simple statement.

Officially opened, The Hall was ready to welcome fans. Besides dignitaries from the hockey community, Toronto Mayor June Rowlands was on hand, as was Metro Chairman Allan Tonks and Ray Hnatyshyn, Canada's Governor General. Hnatyshyn's attendance was poignant, as it was the country's sixth governor general, Lord Stanley of Preston, whose donation of a trophy in his name in 1892 exponentially increased popularity in the sport.

Scotty Morrison welcomes the crowd to the Great Hall at the 1993 opening, and is about to reveal the wall of Honoured Member plaques in "the cathedral for the icons of hockey."

THE RESOURCE CENTRE

Hockey's Hidden Treasures

There is no doubt that the Hockey Hall of Fame Museum downtown is the showcase of the game's history. However, its equally impressive D.K. (Doc) Seaman Hockey Resource Centre, named for the philanthropist and former Calgary Flames owner in the Lakeshore West district of Toronto, is the storehouse of its riches — meticulously collecting and archiving decades of artifacts.

The Hall first opened its doors at Toronto's Canadian National Exhibition Grounds in 1961, although it wasn't until 1983 that a proper library was created. Maurice 'Lefty' Reid, the curator, had the vision to preserve newspaper articles, photographs, books and other items that would become important pieces in the infinite jigsaw puzzle that told hockey's story.

By the mid-1980s, a government grant was used to begin cataloguing artifacts and the library's collection, which would soon stretch across almost the entire second floor of The Hall building at the CNE.

After the move downtown, the archives and a library were situated on the concourse level in what today is the World of Hockey Zone. The collection had the floor space it needed, but not for long. With renewed attention in The Hall thanks to the opening of the Yonge and Front location, the donations of artifacts, photographs and books poured in, compromising the space.

By 1998, the Resource Centre was moved to the second floor of BCE Place, but The Hall was forced to get creative in order to store the multitude of donations, including books, magazines, clippings, photographs and videos, while keeping up to speed with the paperwork and exhibit rotations that accompany newly donated items.

A new facility was needed.

Lakeshore Lions Arena, also known as the Mastercard Centre for Hockey Excellence, opened on September 8, 2009. Since September 2011, the facility has been owned and operated by Lakeshore Arena Corporation, controlled by the City of

Hall of Fame principals congregate at the site for the new Resource Centre. *(Left to right)* Craig Baines, Jeff Denomme, Jim Gregory (NHL), Bill Hay, Mark Grimes (city councillor for Etobicoke-Lakeshore Ward; HHOF board member), Scotty Morrison and Phil Pritchard.

Honoured Members Darryl Sittler *(left)* and Johnny Bower *(right)* flank Bobby Seaman, son of Doc Seaman, at the opening of the Resource Centre on September 8, 2009.

Paper collectibles over the years are carefully preserved in the Resource Centre.

Toronto. The Mastercard Centre has proven to be a vibrant facility addressing the needs of the community while enjoying the marquee value of serving as the practice rink for the Toronto Maple Leafs and Toronto Marlies as well as the home of the Toronto Furies, Faustina Sports Club, Etobicoke Dolphins, Hockey Canada Regional Centre, NHL Alumni Association, the Etobicoke Sports Hall of Fame and the expansive Hockey Hall of Fame Resource Centre.

On the same day that the Mastercard Centre opened, Bill Hay, chairman of The Hall , was joined by Bobby Seaman, son of the late 'Doc' Seaman, as well as Maple Leaf greats Johnny Bower and Darryl Sittler, to cut the ribbon, officially opening the D.K. (Doc) Seaman Hockey Resource Centre in honour of one of the founding owners of the Calgary Flames. Seaman had passed away on January 11, 2009, at the age of 86.

"We are thrilled to be a key partner in this wonderful new complex that provides much needed space to expand and preserve our valuable museum collections," said Hay. "I am especially proud of our association with the Seaman family through which this tribute to an outstanding Canadian and benefactor of grass roots hockey development in this country is made possible."

The Resource Centre is also home to thousands of feet of historical film.

THE SOURCE OF THE RESOURCE CENTRE

In the latter part of the 1990s, the Lakeshore Lions Club discussed adding a second rink to the outdated Lakeshore Lions Arena, built in 1951. The Town of Etobicoke suggested that with ice time at a premium, it would be prudent for the Lions Club to consider a much larger idea. The vacant lot that had once housed Gilbey's Distillery was available. While the property was owned by the Toronto District School Board (TDSB), a land swap was possible. It would allow the Lions Club to build a larger complex.

The service group began discussing a three-rink complex, but a business consultant suggested that a four-pad complex would not only better serve the needs of the community but would be more cost-effective: more rinks means more ice rentals, which would make it easier to pay down the debt. The community got involved and lobbied the Lions Club to go with the four-pad suggestion – three NHL-sized rinks and one Olympic-sized pad. It would be the first new arena built in Toronto in more than a quarter-century.

The deal was complex, and involved a great deal of deliberation between the Lions Club, the TDSB and the city, but after negotiations were completed, the facility was approved. The main level of the arena would include four ice pads with seating, a pro-shop and a snack bar. The second floor would include a restaurant along with office and meeting space.

The Lions Club already had the Toronto Maple Leafs practising at Lakeshore Lions Arena, and there were productive discussions that indicated that Maple Leaf Sports and Entertainment (MLSE) wanted a world-class practice facility and would be involved if the four-pad complex was built. They committed to being involved, with two of the practice rinks to be used by MLSE – one for the Maple Leafs and one for the Leafs American Hockey League affiliate, the Toronto Marlies.

The timing couldn't have been better. The Hall had been in the process of looking to relocate its Resource Centre at the time. Various possibilities were investigated, and The Hall had been in discussions with MLSE about locations for various endeavours when news of the new arena and its availability was announced.

The Hall's Resource Centre opened with the complex in 2009.

The Resource Centre was funded, in part, by contributions from the Seaman Hotchkiss Hockey Foundation, the International Ice Hockey Federation (IIHF), the Department of Canadian Heritage and 10 individuals who formed the 'HRCA Founders Committee.'

At almost 10 times the storage capacity of its previous location, the Resource Centre gave The Hall a space the size of an airplane hangar to access, catalogue, preserve and store items not on display in downtown Toronto, and contributed to making the Outreach Program much more robust.

When visitors tour the Resource Centre, it never fails that an audible gasp is heard when they step through the door and are greeted by a view of the world's largest hockey stick collection. At any given time, the racks hold up to 4,000 sticks, all carefully tagged with the name of the players who used them, his or her team, the date and the stick's significance. All of the sticks have been donated by players and teams of all levels.

Visiting researchers are equally thrilled to find the world's largest collection of hockey resource materials, systematically stored in eleven 15-foot-long 'stacks.' On file are more than 26,000 books, programs and media guides, no fewer than 10,000 individual player files, approximately 9,600 individual team, league and trophy files, and at least 450 binders of hockey cards, tickets and team schedules.

In a climate-controlled room to better preserve the images sits the world's largest photo archive devoted solely to hockey. The 'Cold Room' contains more than two million negatives and slides, 32,000 photographs and prints, and more than 4,000 film reels archived in seven 17-foot-long stacks.

The Digital Archive Centre is used to scan photos, negatives and slides. Resource Centre staff are equipped with photo-editing software and state-of-the-art scanners and printers. The Hall's Images On Ice website (imagesonice.net) alone has more than a million digital images available for the media, publishers and licensees.

Virtually anything associated with the history of hockey is collected, catalogued and preserved by The Hall.

During a 2017 team visit, Sidney Crosby, captain of the Pittsburgh Penguins, studies a few of the hockey-themed paintings that have been collected by The Hall.

The investment in equipment and knowledge resources for the Resource Centre — upgrades in techniques, conservation, preservation and restoration are regularly made — has given The Hall the ability to digitize photography and film and to administer content management systems. This has not only translated into long-term savings, but has also helped create a new revenue source, as organizations and other museums are now able to secure the services of The Hall for their own needs.

In addition to serving thousands of correspondents, media, administrators, teams, players, fans, students, teachers, museums and libraries each year, the Resource Centre is the fabric of the Hall of Fame, playing an integral role in the planning and development of The Hall's exhibition, outreach, fundraising and charitable activities.

The Hall prides itself on having hockey's premier Resource Centre. The extensive collection is possible only through the generous donations from players and their families, teams and the public.

More than 26,000 books about the game have been collected and filed at the Resource Centre, ready for use by researchers.

HONOURED MEMBERS

In a Class of Their Own

GO RIGHT IN!

The original Hall by-laws specified a five-year wait before being eligible for induction, mirroring the election rules of the Baseball Hall of Fame. That was amended in 1968, and there is now a three-year waiting period before eligibility. Over the years, though, there have been 10 exceptions, for exceptional players, who were inducted immediately after retirement, the waiting waived by the Selection Committee.

Dit Clapper | 1947

Maurice Richard | 1961

Ted Lindsay | 1966

Red Kelly | 1969

Terry Sawchuk | 1971

Jean Béliveau | 1972

Gordie Howe | 1972

Bobby Orr | 1979

Mario Lemieux | 1997

Wayne Gretzky | 1999

Discussions about eliminating the waiving of the waiting period had been ongoing for several years, but following Gretzky's induction in 1999, it was the right time to end the practice. The board of directors removed the possibility of immediately ushering a player into The Hall except under "certain humanitarian circumstances."

There was also a consensus among the board that all Honoured Members should have equal status and that their induction would have greater impact and meaning after waiting a few years beyond the "limelight" of their active playing careers.

powerful person in hockey, having made his name as Orr's agent for his first NHL contract. He was also the catalyst behind the the NHLPA in 1967 and was appointed executive director.

Eagleson not only oversaw the NHLPA and its 480 members, but also his own player agency of more than 140 players. He was also instrumental in several high-profile hockey events, including the 1972 Summit Series and the 1976 Canada Cup. Despite his contributions, evidence revealed a shocking amount of criminal or unethical behaviour over the years. He pled guilty to mail fraud in a Boston court in 1998 and was fined $1 million. He pled guilty to three more counts of fraud in Canada, which led to an 18-month jail sentence and disbarment. Honoured Members called for Eagleson's removal from The Hall.

"I challenge the Hockey Hall of Fame to remove Alan Eagleson," announced Brad Park at a media conference. "And if they do not, I will request that I be removed."

The Hall's by-laws didn't account for the removal of an Honoured Member, but after achieving the necessary amendments, Eagleson's fate seemed certain; a vote was scheduled for March 31, 1998. It wouldn't be necessary: He resigned six days prior becoming the first member of any North American sports hall of fame to do so.

The Hall's new location in downtown Toronto was officially opened on June 18, 1993, and six months later, on November 16, the first induction ceremony took place in the spectacular Great Hall with a wonderful backdrop of Honoured Member plaques.

While it was a glorious new beginning for inductions, it wasn't without its own controversy, this time surrounding the election of Gil Stein to the Builder Category. Stein had served as General Counsel for the NHL since 1977 before replacing John Ziegler as NHL president in October 1992. Simultaneously, the league searched for a commissioner, selecting Gary Bettman, who assumed the newly-created position in February 1993.

Stein had replaced several members of the board two weeks prior to their March 1993 meeting, meaning a quarter of the board would consist of persons receiving NHL salaries. Scotty Morrison and David Taylor, both employed by The Hall but paid by the league, expressed concern. The board also decided to change the voting procedure, with the election of nominees requiring a simple majority rather than the previous 75 percent, and rather than secret ballot, the election would be conducted by a show of hands.

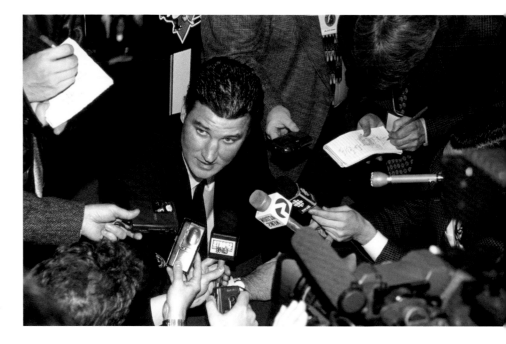

Bruce McNall, chairman of the board, submitted a nomination for the election of Stein. The nomination had been prepared by Stein himself, who had asked McNall to simply sign and submit it. A vote was taken and Stein was elected. There was an immediate hue and cry, suggesting that Stein had orchestrated his own election. Facing a controversy regarding improprieties, NHL Commissioner Bettman engaged independent counsel to investigate. The counsel issued a report, stating that Stein had "improperly manipulated the process of nomination and election to The Hall to assure his election." He withdrew his election and was not inducted.

The incident resulted in several recommendations from counsel, including that the election of builder candidates be delegated to the Selection Committee and that employees, including the chairman and president, be compensated by The Hall, and not by the NHL. League representation on the board remained at seven, but the overall membership increased to 18 from 12 to allow for corporate and government representation, as well as hockey organizations representing the game at various levels.

While the Stein episode sparked widespread and unwanted media attention during The Hall's move to its new location, the impact of the independent counsel report initiated The Hall's autonomy and corporate governance practices that continues to this day.

If the early part of the 1990s had The Hall navigating through the distractions of the Stein affair, the latter part of the decade saw it riding a wave of superstardom. Two of the game's giants were about to enter.

First up, Number 66.

There was no doubt that Mario Lemieux would be elected to The Hall when his career concluded, but, unfortunately, that came sooner than many expected. When injuries and illness forced him to retire in 1997 at age 31, Lemieux was poised to enter The Hall, the waiving of his three-year waiting period guaranteed. To the astonishment of the hockey world, he would return to play again three-and-a-half years later and played parts of five more seasons. (Only Gordie Howe and Guy Lafleur also returned to play in the NHL following their inductions.)

Lemieux's induction was so special that some fans began lining up at 2:00 am for a signing that was to take place mid-afternoon. As he entered the room to begin the autograph session, fans screamed like he was a rock star. One man, who had been waiting for at least 12 hours, finally got his turn. He approached Lemieux and said, "I don't want anything signed. I just want to shake your hand to thank you for everything you did for Pittsburgh." Lemieux offered to sign something for him but he said, "No, I just wanted the opportunity to shake your hand." Lemieux asked Hall staff to get him a Pittsburgh jersey from the store, signed it for the man, and a staff member was able to chase after the man to make certain he received the gift.

Next up, Number 99.

Two years after the induction of 'Le Magnifique,' The Hall called 'The Great One.' Again, there would be no waiting period. The announcement of Gretzky's retirement was made on April 16 and he played his final game on April 18. The following day, he was to be in Toronto and stopped by to visit The Hall.

Bryan Black, the senior vice-president of marketing at the Hockey Hall of Fame at the time, got a call from Admission. "I think Wayne Gretzky is here."

"There was a long lineup because of the excitement about Wayne's retirement," recalled Black. "About halfway down the concourse in the lineup, there was Wayne Gretzky with his son, lining up to pay to get in The Hall! He was kind of incognito, but I went up to him and said, 'Wayne, come in this way.' He said no, he wanted to enter with his son just like everybody else!"

With the unprecedented interest in Gretzky's induction, there was concern that the ceremony should be moved to a larger venue in order to meet the expected demand for tickets. Hall Chairman Bill Hay and President Jeff Denomme met with Gretzky to discuss the ceremony, but the Great One put The Hall at ease. "I would like to be inducted in the Great Hall like everyone else," he said. On November 22, 1999, The Hall opened the magnificent atrium at BCE Place so that 3,000 more guests could join in celebrating the induction of Wayne Gretzky, Scotty Morrison and Andy Van Hellemond, which still stands as The Hall's most-attended ceremony.

While no two induction ceremonies are the same, virtually all feature a high degree of emotion exhibited by Honourees, sometimes simply due to pride of accomplishment, other times because of memories of family and sacrifice and often times caused by memories of having overcome some of life's challenges. The stories are uniquely their own.

Coach Roger Neilson came to personify perseverance after being diagnosed with multiple myeloma, a blood cancer, during the 1999-2000 NHL season. After undergoing a stem cell transplant in February 2000, he made his way back behind the bench as an assistant with Ottawa and recorded his 1,000th game coaching when Jacques Martin stepped aside for the final two games of the season in 2001-02 to allow him to reach the milestone — one of the classiest moves in hockey history. Neilson was inducted into The Hall in 2002. He succumbed to his illness on June 21, 2003.

Patrick Roy didn't plan on attending the entire induction weekend when he was elected in 2006. He told The Hall that he would arrive for the gala on the Monday night, but would be unable to make it to Toronto earlier because his Quebec Remparts junior team had two games scheduled. Nobody could convince the feisty goaltender to change his mind, except Serge Savard. The Hall-of-Fame defenceman called Roy to tell him that missing the induction weekend would mean depriving his family of this extraordinary experience. Roy acquiesced. The QMJHL games were switched and Roy arrived on the Friday night. When he walked into the Great Hall and saw the Honoured Member plaques of Jean Béliveau, Henri Richard and other greats, Roy was moved. "You have no idea how special the induction weekend is until you get there."

Mark Messier's legendary emotion was on display when discussing his induction in 2007. "With all the talk about the Hall of Fame, when you finally get the phone call, it puts things in perspective. After the phone call (from Selection Committee chair Pat Quinn), I hung up and took a couple of moments and had a few thoughts. When we were getting ready to come here

The Class of 1999 featured *(left to right)* Wayne Gretzky (Player), Scotty Morrison (Builder) and Andy Van Hellemond (Referee/Linesman).

Facing Page

TOP. In 1961, many of the living Honoured Members gathered for a photo at The Hall at the CNE.

BOTTOM. In 1993, several Honoured Members previously inducted celebrated with new inductees *(front row, left to right)* Steve Shutt, Billy Smith, Edgar Laprade and Guy Lapointe.

SETTING THE BAR HIGH

Honoured Member status in The Hall is reserved for the greatest players, builders and on-ice officials in hockey through the years. Their election is determined by a Selection Committee appointed by The Hall's Board of Directors, and follows principles and practices as outlined in The Hall's corporate by-laws.

Soon after the Stanley Cup is awarded each year, the committee meets to consider the merits of the nominated candidates. With this role comes a responsibility that each of the 18 electors undertakes with the utmost professsionalism.The committee's choices, both to elect and not to elect, will be challenged by other voices in hockey from time to time. Naturally, there is an inclination to take aim at the alleged "flaws" in the selection process, which is a common theme for sports halls.

The spirit and intent of The Hall's by-laws regarding nomination and election serves to establish and maintain rational criteria for recognition and, to set and keep the bar at a high level. They also help guide the recruitment of knowledgeable and fair-minded hockey people represented by a broad spectrum of the sport, and to ensure that the committee has access to all relevant information and archival materials to assist in making their decisions. Confidentiality rules help attract the best hockey minds to the committee and encourage candid deliberations, defuse lobbying efforts and other politics of influence, place the focus on those who are successfully elected each year and foster and maintain consistent public communications.

Still, there are certain dynamics of the selection process that inherently generate public debate. Although *bona-fide* "public submissions" are circulated to the Selection Committee, only members of the committee can officially nominate candidates for consideration. In the interest of maintaining the highest standards of excellence and exclusiveness, strict limits are imposed on the number of candidates that can be elected in each category annually, and the number of nominees usually exceeds these limits in any given year. Since the number of eligible candidates multiplies each year (after the mandatory three-year waiting period expires for retired players), and the calibre of first-year eligible candidates fluctuates from year to year, naturally some candidates are successful in their first year of eligibility and others are elected within a few or several years later. The timing of a candidate's election to Honoured Memberships can also be influenced by periodic changes to the composition of the Selection Committee with new insights and perspectives exchanged through their collective deliberations.

All things considered, successful candidates must achieve an affirmative vote of at least three-quarters of the Selection Committee to be elected to Honoured Membership. On that basis, together with the collective dedication, diligence and knowledge of the committee, The Hall preserves the standards of excellence for honouring individuals who have brought special distinction to the game.

THE SELECTION COMMITTEE | 2018

The committee is comprised of a cross-section of hockey professionals, representing players, coaches, executives and media, several of whom have been inducted into The Hall themselves.

John Davidson, Chairman

Jim Gregory, Chairman Emeritus | Builder Category

David Branch

Brian Burke

Colin Campbell

Bob Clarke | Player Category

Marc de Foy

Eric Duhatschek

Michael Farber

Ron Francis | Player Category

Mike Gartner | Player Category

Anders Hedberg

Jari Kurri | Player Category

Igor Larionov | Player Category

Pierre McGuire

Bob McKenzie

David Poile

Luc Robitaille | Player Category

Bill Torrey* | Builder Category

* Bill Torrey was a member of the Selection Committee from June 28, 2007 until his untimely passing on May 2, 2018. Bill's amiable personality, together with his outstanding commitment to The Hall and the game of hockey, will be greatly missed.

(to Toronto) for the weekend, and realizing all the players who would share it, it really started to put the importance of the weekend into perspective."

Messier also referenced an uncle who impacted his life by telling him: "We sail on the wake of those who have gone before us." He then added: "No greater testimony of that is being around the Hall of Fame this weekend and all the great players and the sacrifices they made to make our game the incredible game it is. It's the journey and the people you meet along the way and the life lessons you get from playing an incredible game."

The 2010 induction ceremony was highlighted by Cammi Granato and Angela James, both of whom commented on their status as the inaugural female inductees.

In Granato's speech, she said, "I thank the (Selection) Committee for not only considering us, but believing in us, and accepting us. And understanding that we love the game just as much as the men do. You're changing the face of women's hockey alone by accepting us into this prestigious club."

James was no less appreciative. "This has been a long time coming," she smiled, thanking her mother ("You always found a way to allow me to play, no matter what"), her father, her brothers and sisters, her partner of 16 years, Angela, and their three children, "who made the sacrifices night after night so I

could go out and play the game." Addressing her young children, she added, "You might not understand, but tonight, your mom has climbed a very tall mountain!"

The 2011 induction ceremony included Mark Howe. He was the fourth son to join his father as an Honoured Member in the Player Category of The Hall.

Howe thanked a number of people who had helped advance his career, but saved a special remark for his dad. "I'm going to thank you for being the greatest hockey player ever. I want to thank you for being the husband, the father and the person that you are. You are the role model by which I tried to lead my life. I'm so proud to call you my dad."

Howe had something special in mind. "Just after I retired, you mentioned that you wished I would have worn your number 9 Red Wing jersey for just one game. You've never asked me for anything during your lifetime, so I'd like to honour your request." With the audience standing, he donned a Red Wings jersey, and, turning to face the crowd, including his father, showed the number 9 with 'Howe' on the nameplate. Mark said, "Dad, I love you."

The 2013 induction included Brendan Shanahan, the current president of the Toronto Maple Leafs. The pride in Shanahan's induction certainly extended to his mother, Rosaleen. She had always been an enthusiastic supporter, and told a story about calling sports radio stations when Shanahan was first entering

TOP. Angela James proudly receives her Hall of Fame plaque from Hall Chairman Bill Hay in 2010. Angela and Cammi Granato were the first women to be inducted into the Hockey Hall of Fame.

TOP. Mark Howe fulfills a promise to his father by wearing a Detroit Red Wings jersey with the number 9 made famous by his dad at the 2011 Induction.

the league. "Brendan was on TSN doing a phone interview and he told them that I was the first one he called when he found out he'd been inducted. Then the commentator said, 'Oh yeah, your mother used to call in to the radio station and say, 'I like that Brendan Shanahan. He's a real good player,' but she never said she was your mother!' I guess they all knew it was me the whole time because of my Irish accent."

Bill Hay was part of the induction Class of 2015. It was a different role for Bill, who had enjoyed a 33-year affiliation with The Hall, first as a member of the Selection Committee and, in the final 15 years, as chairman and CEO. He was most gracious in receiving Honoured Membership in the Builder Category to recognize the roles he played in partnering Hockey Canada and the CAHA, supporting grassroots development in association with the original owners of the Calgary Flames and his long-time contributions to The Hall.

Rogie Vachon's 2016 induction came 34 years after playing his final NHL game. While it was one of the greatest days of his professional life, the induction had bittersweet moments for the great goaltender. "There is someone very dear missing," he explained in his speech. "I just lost my wife Nicole." A roommate had set them up, and Rogie knew that she was 'the one' the

moment he saw her. They were married in November 1971, and after 44 years of marriage, she died from cancer in February 2016, just nine months before Rogie's induction. "Sometimes, it's not fair," he said in his speech. "She should be here. We spent 45 years together." He concluded with a tender moment addressed to his beloved wife: "I'll see you on the other side."

After an outstanding career, Danielle Goyette became the fifth woman inducted into The Hall when she was elected in 2017. The entire induction weekend left Danielle wide-eyed, but the gala was especially astonishing to her. Honorees are picked up from their hotels by limousine and led by a police procession to The Hall where they are greeted by Chairman of the Board Lanny McDonald and John Davidson, chair of the Selection Committee. They then proceed along the red carpet with spotlights announcing their arrival, and with fans lining the carpet shouting congratulations and snapping photos. Beaming, Goyette's sister announced, "All weekend, I feel like I'm with Céline Dion!"

Once in a while, an induction ceremony has offered an Honoured Member the opportunity to connect with a fan on whose life they've had an impact. There's no greater example of that than Paul Kariya's Hall induction in 2017.

A 28-year-old woman, diagnosed with breast cancer in 2010, had been inspired by the play of Kariya, who had battled through the words of naysayers who had told him that he was too small to play in the NHL. At the time of her diagnosis, she mailed a letter to Kariya detailing her battle with cancer and explaining how she had drawn inspiration from his terrific career. Kariya responded to the young woman with an autographed photo and a note: "See it in your mind, believe in your heart that it is possible and commit to it with every action you take."

The woman had expressed the wish that she'd love to see him play just one more time, but Kariya had played his final NHL game on April 10, 2010. When it was announced that he was to be inducted into The Hall in 2017, the woman's brother contacted The Hall, hoping to be able to get his sister to meet Kariya. Her cancer was in remission, and she had often spoken of the words Kariya had written to her, helping her through her cancer journey.

Kelly Masse, director of corporate and media relations with The Hall, responded, inviting the woman and her brother to the Fan Forum during the induction weekend, an opportunity for fans to interact with inductees. She stood, hesitated for a moment before addressing Kariya, and then detailed her story, tagging the conversation by saying, "Thank you for taking the time to help me keep going. I did, and I'm here today."

The crowd at the Fan Forum applauded wildly, and few had dry eyes. Kariya responded, "We're entertainers, but when you can touch somebody's life in some small way, it means something." He stepped from the stage and gave the woman a hug. The cancer survivor then got her original wish to see Kariya play one more time when he pulled on his equipment for the Haggar Hockey Hall of Fame Legends Classic. It was the first game he had played since retiring.

Truly honourable members.

Facing Page

A delighted young fan meets a hockey hero during an Induction Weekend signing.

TOP. Paul Kariya, a member of the Class of 2017, is embraced by a woman who was inspired by a letter the newly inducted Honoured Member wrote to her after she was diagnosed with cancer.

HONOURED MEMBERS. PERIOD.

On June 27, 2007, The Hall's Selection Committee unanimously passed a resolution for submission to the board of directors, which stated, in part:

With respect to player candidates for Honoured Membership, the same criteria used for men should apply to women. That is, a female candidate would have to be an elite athlete, achieving at the highest level against international and/or professional competition. She would have to sustain excellence in the game over a prolonged period while equaling or exceeding the achievements of the most elite female players of her generation and those who came before her.

On March 31, 2009, the board amended The Hall's by-laws to implement a new voting procedure on the premise that (i) male and female player candidates ought not compete on the same ballot for limited places of Honoured Membership (given the annual limit on the number of inductees who could be elected in the Player Category) and (ii) greatness is and always has been a relative concept and it should be measured against one's peers.

With the amendment in place, the new voting procedure paved the way for the first female inductees in the Player Category to be honoured and recognized alongside male players, and not separately.

In a milestone 2010 ceremony, Cammi Granato *(above)* and Angela James were the first two women inducted into The Hall.

WAYNE

GRETZKY, WHO?

Prior to the 2016-17 NHL season, Wayne Gretzky was introduced as the National Hockey League's Centennial ambassador. He was an easy choice.

Apart from holding or sharing 61 NHL records and having his famous "99" retired league-wide, Gretzky was inducted into the Hockey Hall of Fame in 1999 after The Hall waived its three-year waiting period following retirement for the final time. At the media conference to celebrate the start of the NHL's centennial in 2016, Gretzky recalled one of his many visits to The Hall, this time, with his son Tristan.

"He was 11 or 12. I had a hat on and I went into the Hall of Fame and just told him, 'Keep your head down.'"

Gretzky is as wide-eyed as any visitor to The Hall, soaking up the game's history. "We walked around for two hours and saw everything there was to see."

Spending a fair bit of time in the Great Hall with the Stanley Cup, the other NHL trophies and the Honoured Member plaques, father and son examined the artifact displays before visiting the interactive area, where Tristan wanted to try his hand shooting against the computer-simulated goaltenders. "We went down to the part where you can interact, take some shots. My son got out there and he was four for five. And he said, 'Dad, try it,' so I said, 'Okay.'"

The 'Great One' selected a stick from the rack and took his turn. "I got out there and I missed the first three shots I took." By this point, both Gretzky and those in attendance at the media conference had started chuckling. "The young man who was taking care of the line, walked over to me and said, 'Sir, if you move your hand down the stick a little bit farther...'"

Gretzky, smiling broadly, turned around and lifted his hat. "I said, 'Go get me one of those pucks that are in there.'" He was looking towards the display that included the net into which he scored the goal that broke Gordie Howe's NHL goal-scoring record, a net filled with 802 pucks.

"My son killed himself laughing, and I got out of there!"

As the guffaws slowly died down, Gretzky tagged his anecdote, stating, "I love every part of the Hockey Hall of Fame. It's heaven to me. I love it there." He signed his image on the wall outside the TSN Theatre, adding: "The Best Place in The World."

The Best Place in The World

Wayne Gretzky 99   Dec 2013

THE STANLEY CUP

At Home in the Hall

It's telling that even when a visiting team wins the NHL championship on 'away ice,' the home-side fans will remain in the arena to witness the Stanley Cup presentation despite their club's loss. Likewise, no visitor to the Hall of Fame would ever think of leaving the building without first viewing the Cup. Hockey's famous trophy possesses an almost magical power of attraction wherever it travels and certainly while at its home in The Hall.

The Stanley Cup is the most important artifact and most dominant feature of The Hall. Donated in 1892 by Canada's sixth governor general, Lord Stanley of Preston (who is an Honoured Member of the Hall of Fame in the Builder Category), its actual name is the Dominion Hockey Challenge Cup, but it has carried its Stanley moniker since it was first awarded to the Montreal Hockey Club of the Montreal Amateur Athletic Association (MAAA) in 1893.

As much as fans may recognize it and seek it out when given the special opportunity, there are many misconceptions about the Cup.

There are three versions of the game's greatest trophy. The original Stanley Cup (bowl) is the one donated by Lord Stanley, and due to its age and fragility, has been retired and is on permanent display in the vault in the Great Hall. Then there's the Presentation Cup, which is the only one that ever leaves The Hall. This is the version awarded to the captain of the NHL's championship team by the league's commissioner, and also travels with members of the winning team as they enjoy a day with the historic trophy. Finally, the Exhibition Cup takes centre stage at The Hall when the Presentation Cup is on the road.

Every day, the Cup is reverently positioned in its place of honour in the Great Hall so that visitors can experience the joy of viewing it, touching it, kissing it and getting their picture taken with it. Fans are well aware of the superstitions surrounding the Cup, including that it's bad luck to actually

Lord Stanley, the sixth Canadian governor general, committed to the donation of a trophy for Canada's championship hockey team. He would return to Liverpool before seeing the Cup awarded for the first time.

The inaugural winners of the Stanley Cup (officially named the Dominion Hockey Challenge Cup) were the Montreal Hockey Club, playing under the umbrella of the Montreal Amateur Athletic Association, in 1893.

touch the trophy for anyone who hasn't actually won it. (Do it, and you'll never win it.) Players are particularly adept at getting close to the Cup, but won't dare lay a finger on its shiny surface.

What sets the Stanley Cup apart from the trophies of other major sports? Certainly its age. At 126 years (in 2018), it is the grandfather of all major sports trophies — while still looking great for its years. And whereas Major League Baseball, the National Football League and the National Basketball Association mint new championship trophies each year, the Stanley Cup is the only one among the majors presented as an original. Teams may win it, but they know that it is borrowed and that their claim to the Cup must be defended again the following season.

A CLASSY GESTURE

During the summer of 2005, the Stanley Cup was brought to past winners who never had the opportunity to spend time with it, including Glenn Hall, Ted Lindsay and Frank Mahovlich.

A Stanley Cup winner in 1961, Hall had never even had the chance to hoist the Cup. So in July 2005, he welcomed it to his Stony Plain, Alberta home and, surrounded by family and friends, raised hockey's most prized trophy over his head for the first time — more than 44 years since he first earned the right to do so.

The Cup was an honoured guest at the (Frank)Mahovlich home, above, and happily hoisted by Glenn Hall, opposite, in the summer of 2005.

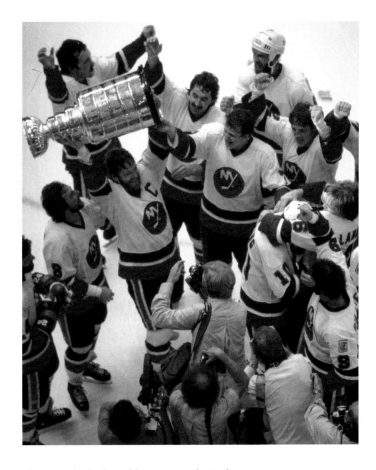

The New York Islanders celebrate winning the Stanley Cup in one of their four consecutive championships that began in 1980. Honoured Members Mike Bossy, Clark Gillies, Denis Potvin, Billy Smith and Bryan Trottier were key parts of the Islanders dynasty.

HOIS

There is no greater dream for a professional hockey player than to raise the Stanley Cup as NHL champion. That's just the start. Every year upon presentation of the trophy to the championship team, a summer of celebration begins, as each of the organization's players and staff enjoy a day with the Stanley Cup — a tradition which has no rival in any sport. The Cup has travelled around the world, including stays in Russia, Japan and Switzerland, and some two dozen other countries.

The Cup enjoys rock star status wherever it travels, including to concerts, backyard barbecues and seats of government. It has been brought to beaches, mountaintops and the Arctic, and spent numerous nights in clubs, pubs and hot tubs. It has been a chalice for champagne and beer, and a bowl for cereal and oats (race horses have eaten from it). It has even held babies for christening. (In 1996, Sylvain Lefebvre of the Colorado Avalanche had his child baptized in the special font.)

In 2009, Pittsburgh Penguins star Sidney Crosby brought the Cup back to his hometown of Cole Harbour, Nova Scotia. The Canadian Armed Forces provided a Sea King helicopter, which flew the conquering hero and his prize to the nearby Halifax Dockyard where they landed on the flight deck of the HMCS *Preserver*. Crosby and his entourage toured Halifax, getting scenic shots with the Cup all around one of Canada's oldest cities. The group then returned to Cole Harbour where an estimated 75,000 jammed the streets for a parade. Mayor Peter Kelly welcomed Crosby, and thanked him for putting Cole Harbour on the world map. He then declared August 7, 2009 as 'Sidney Crosby Day,' and the crowd went wild.

In 2012, the Stanley Cup travelled to Slovenia — the 24th country on its world tour at the time. Los Angeles Kings star Anze Kopitar played host as the Cup sailed by boat on Lake Bled and toured his hometown of Hrusica.

TING THE CUP

The Cup also uniquely carries the names of each of the championship team's players and key personnel, engraved into its silver patina for all time. Finally, the Stanley Cup belongs to the fans. It is openly displayed at The Hall or while in its travels around the world and not sequestered in a display case. Fans are encouraged to approach it and experience it like a winning captain might — touching aside.

Neither fans nor players have lost their excitement for the Cup over the years. "No matter whether it's little kids or adults playing a kids' game, the reaction is the same," says Phil Pritchard, formally the vice-president of the Resource Centre and curator of the Hockey Hall of Fame, and informally the 'Keeper of the Cup' while it's on the road. "Whether the Stanley Cup is visiting a player's hometown, is taken to a hospital or is seen by fans in the Great Hall of the Hockey Hall of Fame, it is the greatest feeling in the world to know that the trophy makes someone smile. Everyone has a special place in their heart for the Stanley Cup."

Here are some noteworthy Stanley typos.

1937-38 | **Chicago Black Hawks** *Pete Palangio's name appears twice, once spelled correctly and once incorrectly as PALAGIO.*

1941-42 | **Toronto Maple Leafs** *Turk Broda is represented twice, once as* TURK BRODA *and once as* WALTER BRODA.

1946-47 | **Toronto Maple Leafs** *Gaye Stewart is misspelled as* GAVE STEWART.

1951-52 | **Detroit Red Wings** *Coach Tommy Ivan's name is misspelled as* TOMMY NIVAN; *Alex Delvecchio's name is misspelled as* ALEX BELVECCHIO.

1956-60 | **Montreal Canadiens** *Jacques Plante won the Stanley Cup five consecutive years, his name is spelled differently each and every time.*

1962-63 | **Toronto Maple Leafs** *Misspelled as* TORONTO MAPLE LEAES.

1971-72 | **Boston Bruins** *Misspelled as* BQSTQN BRUINS.

1974-75 | **Montreal Canadiens** *Bob Gainey's name is misspelled as* GAINY.

1980-81 | **New York Islanders** *Misspelled as* NEW YORK ILANDERS.

1983-84 | **Edmonton Oilers** *Owner Peter Pocklington included the name of his father, Basil Pocklington, who was not affiliated with the team. The NHL learned of the move and ordered the name removed. The name is now covered by 16 X's.*

1995-96 | **Colorado Avalanche** ADAM DEADMARSH *was misspelled as* ADAM DEADMARCH. *It was later corrected (a Stanley Cup first).*

2001-02 | **Detroit Red Wings** MANNY LAGASE *was corrected to* MANNY LEGACE.

2005-06 | **Carolina Hurricanes** ERIC STAAAL *was corrected to* ERIC STAAL.

2009-10 | **Chicago Blackhawks** KRIS VERTSEEG *was corrected to* KRIS VERSTEEG.

NEW YORK ILANDERS 1980-81
PRES. & GEN. MGR.

There have been numerous alterations to the Cup's structure. In its infancy, tiered rings were added to the bottom of the bowl, followed by long, narrow bands in 1927 and uneven bands in '47. The bands are often retired to make room for the names of new champions. Retired bands, along with the original Stanley Cup bowl, are proudly displayed in Lord Stanley's Vault in the Great Hall. Currently, the Cup consists of a bowl, three tiered bands, a collar, and five barrel or uniform bands. The trophy stands at 35¼ inches and weighs 34½ pounds.

EVOLUTION OF THE

1893-1920s | DOMINION HOCKEY CHALLENGE CUP

The first Stanley Cup-winning team was the Montreal Hockey Club in 1893.

EARLY 1920s | THE ORIGINAL BOWL WITH TIERS

The Ottawa Senators of the 1920s are considered the NHL's first dynasty. The team won four Stanley Cup championships through the decade, starting with their victory over the Seattle Metropolitans in 1920.

FROM PUNCH BOWL TO HOLY GRAIL

The original Stanley Cup was crafted from a silver punch bowl purchased on behalf of Sir Frederick Arthur Stanley, Lord Stanley of Preston and son of the Earl of Derby in 1892 for 10 guineas ($50.00). The G.R. Collins and Company of Sheffield, England, was commissioned by Lord Stanley to engrave an inscription on the Cup: "From Stanley of Preston" - "Dominion Hockey Challenge Cup."

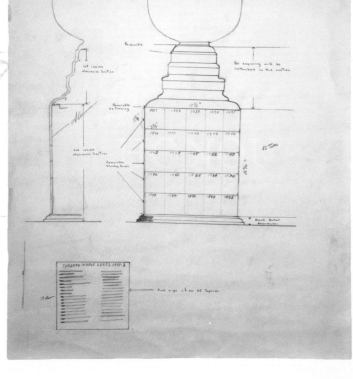

As the 'Stovepipe' Cup began to grow unwieldy, silversmith Carl Poul Petersen designed a new shape for the trophy.

1926 | The Stanley Cup becomes the official championship trophy of the NHL

1946 | After two decades of NHL action, the 'Stovepipe Cup' had grown very tall. The NHL commissioned world-famous silversmith Carl Poul Petersen to re-design the trophy.

1963 | The original Cup (bowl) was retired to The Hall because it had become thin and fragile.

1968 | Petersen was commissioned to create a 'presentation' version of the Cup.

1993 | An additional replica of the Cup was made by Montreal silversmith Louise St. Jacques. It sits in The Hall when the Presentation Cup is unavailable.

1927-47 | THE 'STOVEPIPE' STANLEY CUP

The 1936-37 Detroit Red Wings, led by coach Jack Adams, celebrate with the Vezina Trophy won by Normie Smith, the 'Stovepipe' Stanley Cup and the Prince of Wales Trophy for their first-place finish in the NHL's American Division.

1950s-PRESENT | THE STANLEY CUP

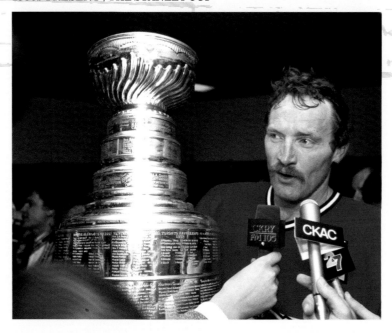

The 1970s were incredible years for the Montreal Canadiens, with a defence that included Larry Robinson (pictured). They won the Stanley Cup six times through the decade.

SHOW STANLEY SOME LOVE!

As much as the Cup is cherished and revered by winning teams today, there have been examples in hockey's colourful past when the championship trophy wasn't always treated with white gloves — including by those who won it!

In 1924, members of the Montreal Canadiens, on their way to a victory party, stored the Stanley Cup in the trunk of their car. On their way to the festivities, the vehicle suffered a flat tire. The players removed the Cup from the trunk to get at the spare, changed the tire, but drove off, leaving the Stanley Cup sitting on a snowbank. When it came time to drink Champagne from the Cup, they discovered that they didn't have it with them, so they roared back to where they changed the tire and, thankfully, the Cup was still there.

After a night of celebrating their Stanley Cup victory in 1905, members of the Ottawa Silver Seven felt it necessary to see if one could kick the Cup onto Ottawa's frozen Rideau Canal. One of them lined it up and gave it a boot, drop-kick style. In a true test of his accuracy and distance, the Cup landed on the canal's ice and skidded across the surface. That established, the boys went on their merry way and the Cup sat on the ice until the next day when sober heads prevailed and Lord Stanley's mug was rescued. It was then placed in the capable hands of Harry Smith, a Silver Seven member.

After the traditional Stanley Cup parade honouring the 1979 Montreal Canadiens, star forward Guy Lafleur impulsively grabbed the Stanley Cup and placed it in the trunk of his car. He then drove to his parents' house in Thurso, Quebec, where he displayed the Cup on the front lawn and allowed friends and family to photograph and enjoy the trophy. While Thurso residents enjoyed the prank, the men responsible for the Cup's safety were searching frantically for the missing prize. Lafleur returned the Cup later that night, but was told never to repeat his stunt.

In 1907, the Montreal Wanderers left the Cup at the home of a photographer they hired to document their trophy win. The photographer's mother decided it would make a wonderful flower pot, and it served that purpose for a few months until the Wanderers brass remembered and rescued it from the earthly grave.

NHL players are not the only ones who've dreamt of getting their hands on the Stanley Cup. On at least three occasions, thieves have tried to make off with hockey's greatest prize, only to come away empty-handed like a playoff team with weak goaltending.

Crooks broke into The Hall building on the grounds of the CNE on April 9, 1969, and despite an elaborate alarm system, smashed a display case with a shovel and made off with the Hart Memorial Trophy (regular season MVP), the Conn Smythe Trophy (playoff MVP), the Calder Memorial Trophy (rookie of the year) and approximately 100 skating medals. They passed on taking the Prince of Wales Trophy (East Division champs), the Art Ross Trophy (regular season points leader), the James Norris Memorial Trophy (best defenceman) and — of course — the Lady Byng Memorial Trophy (most gentlemanly player).

It was suspected that the target of the hockey hoodlums was the Stanley Cup, but fortunately, the famous trophy was not in the museum at the time. NHL President Clarence Campbell, outwardly calm, stated that the league would commission new versions of the trophies from Carl Poul Petersen, the silversmith who created the originals. "The trophies have absolutely no value to anyone except their worth in metal," he said.

Detective Harold Lambert of the Metropolitan Toronto Police followed several leads, and was soon able to recover all three trophies, wrapped in green garbage bags, from a garage in nearby Etobicoke, Ontario. No one was charged with the thefts.

In January 1970, the silver collar below the bowl of the Cup, along with the glass case in which it was displayed, were stolen. The collar consisted of the engraved names of the Stanley Cup champions from 1924 (Montreal Canadiens), 1925 (Victoria Cougars) and 1926 (Montreal Maroons). It took seven years, but on September 18, 1977, Sergeant Robert Morrison of Toronto's 54 Division received a call, telling him to go to a dry cleaning shop in Toronto. Constables Gordon Black and William Thompson would find the rings wrapped in brown paper. "It looked like a Christmas package when we picked it up," Sergeant Morrison said.

The 29-year-old proprietor of the shop was charged with possession of stolen property and claimed that the rings had been left at his shop two or three months earlier. Sergeant Morrison later explained, "It hasn't been there (at the dry cleaning shop) for seven years. It's been around the criminal underworld. Several people have had it and the dry cleaning store is where it came to rest."

Apart from a few minor dings, the band was in relatively good condition, although a name had been scratched into the silver beside the names of the Stanley Cup champions. "It's not the right way to get your name on the Stanley Cup," shrugged Lefty Reid, The Hall's curator.

In early December 1970, thieves broke into The Hall for a third time within two years after twisting out the lock cylinder in the east-side door, and made off with the Stanley Cup (presentation version), the Conn Smythe Trophy and the Bill Masterton Memorial Trophy.

Detective Sergeant Wallace Harkness of the Metropolitan Toronto Police answered a call from an anonymous woman, claiming to speak on behalf of the thieves, who demanded that unless a friend who was in prison on a "serious robbery charge" was released, the Cup would be deposited in Lake Ontario. The police refused to bargain, but were concerned that losing the Cup in the lake would be a desecration to hockey's most prestigious award. "That's like burning the flag," Detective Harkness told the media.

Realizing that they had little bargaining power — the Cup would be all but impossible to sell without arousing suspicion — the thieves gave up their treasure. On December 23, 1970, Detective Harkness was aroused from his sleep by a commotion outside his East York, Ontario home. When he went outside to investigate, he found the Stanley Cup the Conn Smythe Trophy and the Masterton Trophy sitting in his driveway. Other than some minor repairs required for the Masterton, the trophies were undamaged.

UPI Telephoto

Back home

Original collar for hockey's Stanley Cup is back in Toronto's Hockey Hall of Fame. It was stolen in January of 1970 and was found Sunday wrapped in brown paper in Toronto cleaning store. Hall curator Maurice Reid returns relic to its pedestal.

(Form 11)
(Section 627)

SUBPOENA TO A WITNESS

HEISTING THE CUP

CANADA
PROVINCE OF ONTARIO
JUDICIAL DISTRICT OF YORK

TO   Maurice Reid
of   135 Lynnbrook Dr.
      Scarborough, Ont.

WHEREAS   Diomed Karrys   (accused)

has been charged that   he on or about the   18th   day of   September   77

the Municipality of Metropolitan Toronto in the Judicial District of York unlawfully did   have possession of

The 'Keepers of the Cup' over the years have included Hall curators Bobby Hewitson (*above*), Phil Pritchard (*right*) and Maurice 'Lefty' Reid (*opposite*).

CUP

Phil Pritchard owns more white gloves than the average person. Then again, he doesn't exactly have an average job.

"Apart from playing in the NHL and competing for the Stanley Cup, which is a dream for hockey fans, there's nothing else I'd rather be doing," said the affable vice-president of the Resource Centre and curator of the Hockey Hall of Fame, a.k.a. 'Keeper of the Cup,' the white-gloved principal who carries the famous trophy to various events, including the Stanley Cup championship.

The white gloves became associated with Cup presentations back in 1993-94, thanks to an idea from The Hall.

"We had a conference call with the league on redesigning the Stanley Cup presentation and incorporating the red carpet treatment and the Hockey Hall of Fame staff," explained Pritchard. "The thought was to have us dress the same in our Hall uniforms, and we suggested wearing our white gloves (to carry the trophy) as we always wear them when handling artifacts. The white gloves were born."

The first red carpet, white glove Stanley Cup presentation was at Madison Square Garden after Game 7 in 1994 (New York vs. Vancouver). The Hall had been part of the presentations in previous years, but not to that magnitude.

Pritchard's Hall of Fame career began when he was one of eight employees at The Hall's CNE location, and as the marketing administrative co-ordinator, he found himself working at reception, in the gift shop and doing anything he could to promote The Hall. Following in the footsteps of Bobby Hewitson and Lefty Reid, as well as James Duplacey and Joe Romain, who served as associate curators following Reid's departure, Pritchard took over curatorial duties in 1991. While his role at The Hall is extensive, he is best known as guardian of hockey's most iconic symbol.

"In October 1988, Jeff Denomme (Hall president and CEO) and I took the Stanley Cup to the Newmarket Minor Hockey Association's annual banquet. People were thrilled. That was the first time I ever held the Stanley Cup."

Since then, Pritchard has been around the world several times, travelling with the Cup more than a hundred days each year. He estimates that he has mailed more than 3,200 postcards to his wife, Diane, from the destinations he's visited. "History is being made every time the Cup goes out, and I am honoured to be part of it," states Pritchard.

He has also become almost as well known as his famous travelling companion, including sharing the spotlight in a couple of TV ad campaigns. "Mom, look! It's the guy with the Cup from the commercial," kids announce, and Pritchard graciously, if not shyly, has his picture taken with the children or shakes their hands. Many want to know where his white gloves are, and he readily pulls a pair out from his pocket. "I go through a lot of gloves each year," Pritchard laughs.

Pritchard estimates that the Stanley Cup has visited 25 countries, always with a Keeper of the Cup. It is all but impossible for him to isolate a single trip as more meaningful than any other, but it was the trophy's first visit to Russia that really galvanized for him just how passionate people around the world are about hockey. "After the Red Wings won the Cup in 1997, plans were made for Igor Larionov, Slava Kozlov and Viacheslav Fetisov to take the Stanley Cup to Russia. When we got there, the players took the Cup off the plane. It was a rainy, dreary day, but there were thousands of people there. Fetisov walked the Cup over to the chain link fence, and people stuck their fingers through it to touch it. It was absolutely amazing! These people really appreciated the legacy of the Stanley Cup. Their reaction was phenomenal!"

Pritchard also plays a significant role in The Hall's relationship with the International Ice Hockey Federation (IIHF). The partnership has expanded exponentially, and he and his team travel extensively to meet with the IIHF, collect artifacts and to serve as the official photographers of the IIHF. The Hall has also digitized the archives of the IIHF, a service also performed for Hockey Canada.

Pritchard also oversees the activities of the D.K. (Doc) Seaman Hockey Resource Centre, a beehive of activity with a small staff that attends as many hockey events as humanly possible, making contacts, arranging for the donation of artifacts and, in many cases, collecting photography to add to an already extraordinary archive. With that comes the need to preserve and catalogue items. The team has been instrumental in building The Hall's collection of hockey artifacts and photographs into the largest in the world.

The perpetually-smiling Pritchard also oversees the outreach program, taking The Hall on the road to meet fans. This can become a logistical nightmare, as Pritchard must serve as a sort of traffic controller, moving trophies, artifacts and employees from city to city, dealing with customs, transportation and personnel to ensure that everything moves smoothly.

And then, there is the non-stop barrage of questions: "Who wore number 4 before Bobby Orr?" (Al Langlois), "Who scored the first goal in Toronto Maple Leafs history?" (George Patterson), and "My grandfather always told me he played for the Detroit Falcons. Can you tell me when he played and do you have a picture of him in uniform?" (We'll look into it and get back to you).

It's all part of the Pritchard white-glove treatment.

WHO OWNS THE STANLEY CUP?

Depends who you ask.

Technically, the famous trophy was donated by Lord Stanley to the fine people of Canada in 1892. Early on, it had been the focus of championship play of both amateur and pro teams, but in 1947, the NHL was granted control of the trophy and only league teams have competed for it since. Actual ownership, however, remains a silver-grey area that has been the focus of debate over the years by passionate parties ranging from beer leaguers to barristers.

Fans can rest assured, however, that the Cup is in good hands, safeguarded while in its home at The Hall and chaperoned *(please see "Keeper of the Cup")* whenever it leaves the building. Further, any decisions regarding the Cup fall to two trustees as outlined by Lord Stanley upon donation who have absolute power over all matters regarding the trophy, including maintaining the rules, governing the competitions and ensuring the Cup is awarded and returned in proper condition. When one trustee resigns or is in need of replacement, the remaining trustee nominates a substitute.

The current Stanley Cup trustees are Ian 'Scotty' Morrison, appointed in 2002, and Brian O'Neill, appointed in 1988, both Honoured Members of The Hall.

The 1906-07 Stanley Cup champion Montreal Wanderers are the only team to have their name engraved within the inner bowl.

The Wanderers were the first team to engrave their roster, also in 1906-07.

Team roster engraving became an annual tradition in 1924.

MOST APPEARANCES ON THE CUP (TEAM)
Montreal Canadiens (24)

MOST CONSECUTIVE APPEARANCES ON THE CUP (TEAM)
Montreal Canadiens (5)

MOST APPEARANCES ON CUP (PLAYER)
Montreal Canadiens | Henri Richard (11), Jean Béliveau (10), Yvan Cournoyer (10), Claude Provost (9), Jacques Lemaire (8), Maurice Richard (8) and Jean-Guy Talbot (7)

Detroit Red Wings, Toronto Maple Leafs | Red Kelly (8)

MOST APPEARANCES ON CUP (COACH)
Scotty Bowman (9) | Detroit Red Wings, Pittsburgh Penguins and Montreal Canadiens
Toe Blake (8) | Montreal Canadiens

FIRST WOMAN ENGRAVED ON CUP
Marguerite Norris | President of the Detroit Red Wings (1954 & 1955)

THE RINGS
It takes 13 years for a ring to fill with names. When all spaces on the rings are full, the top ring is retired to the Hockey Hall of Fame and a new ring is 'rotated in' to the bottom spot. A player's name remains on the Cup for between 50 and 63 years.

A PRICELESS COLLECTION

From Wartime to Warhol

How do you go about building the greatest collection of hockey artifacts in the world? If you're the Hall of Fame, one Stanley Cup ring, Warhol and 'Lucky Loonie' at a time.

"Most artifacts come from family, friends or the players themselves," explains Phil Pritchard, the vice-president, Resource Centre and curator. "We try to stay on top of milestone and unique events, of course, but mainly we're interested in items that tell the story of this great game. We want something special that catches the eye and provides a unique memory for everyone who comes through our doors."

With more than 1,500 items on display at The Hall at any given time, and millions more — when factoring in the renowned photo archive at the Resource Centre — there is certainly a lot to catch the eye of visitors. The collection chronicles the game from first puck drop through the modern era and ensures the exhibits at the museum remain fresh, exciting and engaging for all generations. And for those who can't make it to The Hall, The Hall will make it to them, eventually, thanks to an outreach program that takes it to locations around the world.

"We preserve and conserve every item that gets donated so that it will remain part of our collection forever," explains Pritchard. "Our goal and mandate is to treat them as part of the history of the game, and share them on display or as part of our travelling collection. We sometimes loan artifacts to other museums to promote hockey in their communities, or include them as part of an Education Program we've designed for students and teachers. A lot of good comes from our collection."

Beyond the granddaddy of them all — the Stanley Cup (*please see page 81*) — The Hall's collection includes items that are an important part of hockey's lore, and some as simple as a dollar coin.

At the Winter Olympic Games in Salt Lake City, Utah, in 2002, International Olympic Committee (IOC) officials hired Dan Craig, the NHL's ice-making consultant, to oversee conditions at the E Center Arena. Craig, in turn, hired the ice crew from Edmonton, with whom he had worked so successfully

in previous years, to assist him. One of the crew, Trent Evans, buried a Canadian one-dollar coin, a "loonie" (one side of the coin bears the image of a loon, a bird common to Canada) under the faceoff circle at centre ice for good luck.

Team Canada members from both the women's and men's teams were aware of the good luck talisman, but had been sworn to secrecy. On February 21, when Canada's women edged the USA 3-2 to win gold, they briefly gathered around centre ice but were shooed away so as not to divulge the secret. Three days later, Canada's men triumphed over the Americans, 5-2, to capture the gold medal. At that point, the loonie was chipped out of the ice in celebration for bringing both Canadian teams such good luck.

In the Canadian dressing room following the men's win, photographer Dave Sandford motioned for The Hall's Pritchard to join Wayne Gretzky, Team Canada executive director, for a photo opportunity. Holding the coin, Gretzky shook Pritchard's hand, simultaneously donating the coin to The Hall's collection, whispering, "Don't spend it in a pop machine on the way home."

The legend of the 'Lucky Loonie' was born and the coin was mounted in a display that invited fans to see and touch it (for their own good fortune), drawing lineups in the hundreds and

The Lucky Loonie travelled from Salt Lake City, Utah, to The Hall in 2002 tucked safely in the luggage of Cup Keeper Phil Pritchard. The coin, which had been buried beneath centre ice during Olympic play, was put on display for fans to see and touch for their own good luck.

After winning Olympic gold in 2002, Team Canada members *(left to right)* Thérèse Brisson, Geraldine Heaney and Danielle Goyette look at the 'Lucky Loonie' embedded in the ice at the rink in Salt Lake City.

Facing Page

Rod Gilbert, as interpreted by Andy Warhol.

BOTTOM. The famous Turofsky photo collection is among the highlights of The Hall's three million-plus photo archive.

said. "At first, they didn't get what he was." The Rangers ended up enjoying Warhol's company, and were quite protective of the artist. "We had quite an adventure. It was fun times."

Warhol used synthetic polymer silkscreen ink on 40″-by-40″ canvases. Eight sets, using different colour schemes, were made of each athlete's portrait. Gilbert and his wife, Judy, convinced a collector to donate his Gilbert print to The Hall, where it will remain a famous part of the collection forever.

One of the best known photo collections at The Hall is the Imperial Oil Turofsky Collection. It consists of more than 21,500 photographs (4″-by- 5″ negatives plus glass plates) covering the period from 1890 to the mid-1950s. The photographs were shot primarily by brothers Lou and Nat Turofsky, who extensively chronicled Toronto life for some 50 years through their Toronto-based Alexandra Studio.

The incredible Turofsky collection was purchased for The Hall in 1981 with funds donated by Imperial Oil Limited. Hockey historian Bill Galloway, an archivist with the Public Archives of Canada, has called it "the most comprehensive accumulation of visuals relating to the game of hockey in existence."

While much of the peerless photography focuses on posed and action shots of the Toronto Maple Leafs, the collection includes other NHL teams as well as minor league teams, junior squads and the long-forgotten Toronto Hockey League, a wartime mercantile league.

Long-forgotten leagues, teams and artifacts are often the focus of Hall researches and archivists. Sometimes their efforts pay off, sometimes they don't.

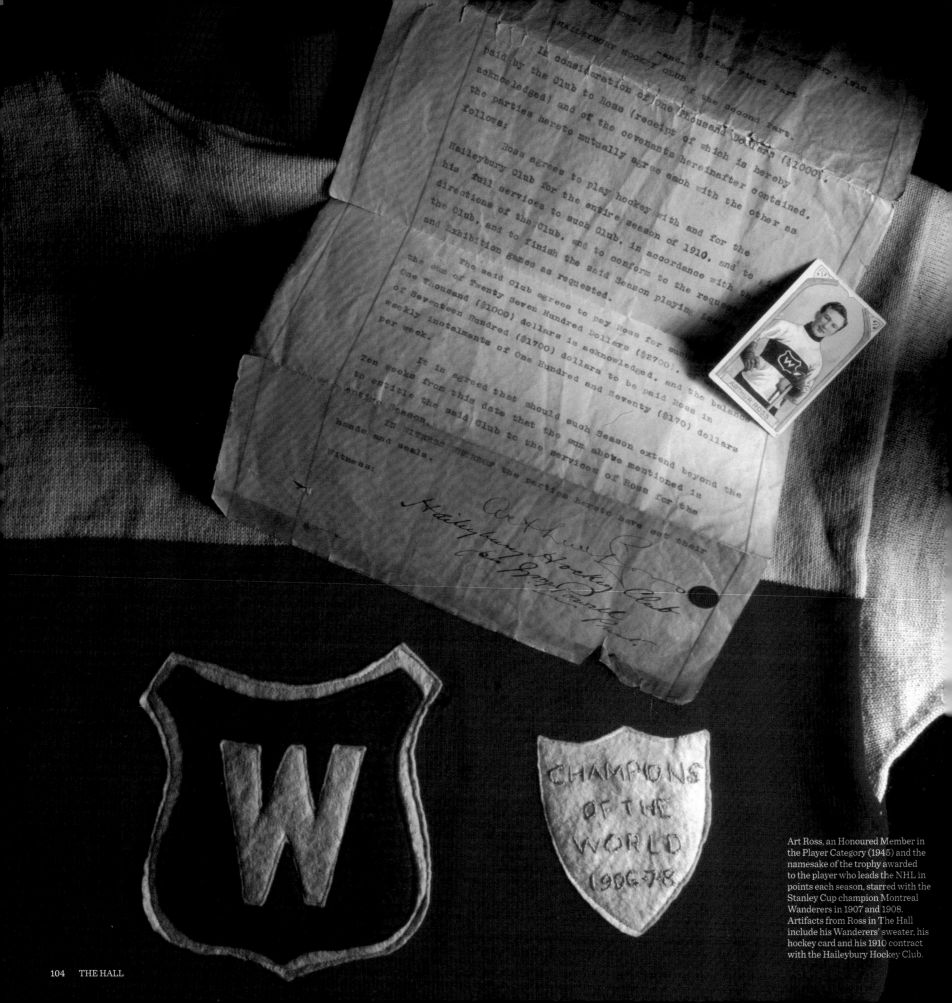

Art Ross, an Honoured Member in the Player Category (1945) and the namesake of the trophy awarded to the player who leads the NHL in points each season, starred with the Stanley Cup champion Montreal Wanderers in 1907 and 1908. Artifacts from Ross in The Hall include his Wanderers' sweater, his hockey card and his 1910 contract with the Haileybury Hockey Club.

NO 36

NEWSY LALONDE of RENFREW CLUB.

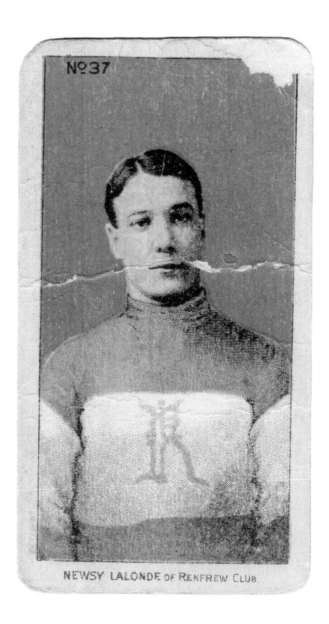

NO 37

NEWSY LALONDE of RENFREW CLUB.

The first set of hockey cards was issued by Imperial Tobacco in 1910. The series featured 36 players, but curiously, Newsy Lalonde of the Renfrew Creamery Kings was issued card #36 as well as card #37! Only three known copies of #37 exist, one of which belongs to The Hall.

3 MINUTES IN TIME

Among the intriguing artifacts in The Hall's collection are the minute books of three leagues that helped provide the foundation for the hockey we enjoy today.

The NHL was born from the ashes of the National Hockey Association. After ongoing disputes with the owner of the Toronto Blueshirts, representatives of the Montreal Canadiens, Montreal Wanderers, Ottawa Hockey Club and Quebec Hockey Club met to discuss the future. The first entry in the minute book tells the story:

At a meeting of representatives of hockey clubs held at the Windsor Hotel, Montreal, November 22nd, 1917, it was explained that in view of the suspension of operations by the National Hockey Association of Canada Limited, a meeting (was called)...to ascertain if some steps could not be taken to perpetuate the game of hockey. Frank Calder was elected to the chair and a discussion ensued, after which it was moved...that the Canadiens, Wanderers, Ottawa and Quebec Hockey Clubs unite to comprise the National Hockey League. It was then moved...that this league agrees to operate under the rules and conditions governing the game of hockey prescribed by the National Hockey Association of Canada Limited.

Quebec almost immediately withdrew and was replaced by the Toronto Arena Hockey Club. From those humble beginnings, the NHL has flourished into the top league in the world with 31 teams across the U.S. and Canada.

At a meeting held December 4, 1914 in Ottawa, Ontario, delegates from across Canada convened to discuss the Allan Cup tournament; in essence, overseeing amateur hockey on a national level. At this meeting, the Allan Cup was selected as the championship trophy for amateur hockey in Canada. This was the initiation of the Canadian Amateur Hockey Association (CAHA). William Northey was named the CAHA's first chairman, and was inducted into The Hall as a Builder in 1947. As the governing body for amateur hockey nationally, the organization added the Memorial Cup to its responsibilities in 1919, designating the Allan Cup for Senior hockey and the Memorial Cup for Junior play. In 1968, the Canadian Hockey Association, or Hockey Canada, was formed to oversee Canada's national teams. By 1994, the CAHA merged with Hockey Canada, using the latter name.

In 1911, Frank Smith played hockey with his high-school friends on the outdoor rinks in The Beach area of Toronto. He coordinated shinny games so that neighbourhoods could compete in an organized league. With Smith serving as secretary, a position he'd hold for 50 years, The Beaches Hockey League was formed with 99 players and five teams. As the league expanded, the name changed from the Toronto Hockey League to the Metropolitan Toronto Hockey League to the current Greater Toronto Hockey League (GTHL), the largest youth hockey organization in terms of members in the world. Smith's vision is preserved in The Beaches Hockey League minute book, and his legacy is enshrined in The Hall in the Builder Category (1962).

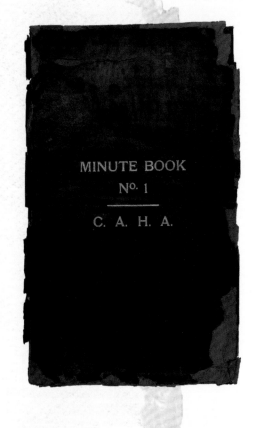

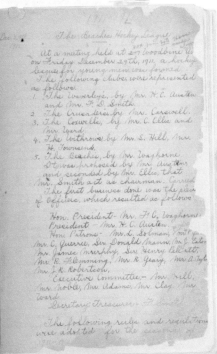

The historic cover of the C. A. H. A. Minute Book is shown above, while a page from The Beaches Hockey League minutes is shown at right.

MINUTE BOOK

NO. 1

CAHA

The Preston Rivulettes dominated women's hockey during the 1930s. Formed in 1930 in Preston, Ontario, (now part of Cambridge, Ontario) they joined the Ladies Ontario Hockey Association (LOHA) in January 1931 and won the league championship, repeating in each of the following nine seasons. Captained by Hilda Ranscombe, the Rivulettes boasted a record (unofficially) unmatched by any hockey team — two losses and three ties in 350-odd games played! In 1998, Dr. Taras Zienchuk of Kitchener, Ontario, donated Ranscombe's gloves, socks, pants and number 5 sweater, all worn during the Rivulettes dynasty, to The Hall.

While the donated equipment tells an important part of the development of the women's game, a key artifact, the Lady Bessborough Trophy — vied for every year by the Rivulettes — remains unaccounted for. The championship trophy, named for the wife of the 14th governor general of Canada, was awarded to the top team in the Dominion Women's Amateur Hockey Association, a league that existed from 1933 to '40. The league folded at the start of the Second World War as many of the women were taking factory positions to support the war efforts. The trophy has yet to be found.

If there is such a thing as a dream artifact on The Hall's wish list it would be a sweater from the Hamilton Tigers, a franchise that was in the NHL from 1920 to '25. After struggling mightily through its first four seasons, the Tigers finished first in 1924-25, but went on strike before the playoffs in a squabble over being paid to compete in the post-season. The owners refused and dissolved the team, selling the players to the New York Americans, who were joining the league that season. So rare is this sweater that in 2010, Russ Boychuk produced a documentary about the search titled *Hunting the Last Hamilton Tiger*.

There was no misplacing, misidentifying or otherwise mistaking the value of the artifacts surrounding an event at New York's Madison Square Garden on April 18, 1999, the night Wayne Gretzky retired from the NHL. The Rangers lost 2-1 in overtime to the Penguins, but all anyone cared about — including curators at The Hall — was the significance of the game, Gretzky's 1,487th in regular season play in which he earned his 1,963rd assist on Brian Leetch's goal for New York.

The striking jersey of the Preston Rivulettes, the team that dominated women's hockey in the 1930s, is part of The Hall's collection.

The World of Hockey Zone at The Hall is an incredible exhibit of hockey's global popularity. National team jerseys include *(left to right)* Finland (Teemu Selänne), Sweden (Börje Salming), Czechoslovakia (Frantisek Cernik), the Soviet Union (Vladislav Tretiak) and Slovakia (Peter Stastny).

With his hair still damp and perspiration dripping from his brow, Wayne Gretzky stripped off his equipment for the final time on April 18, 1999, packed it away and asked that it be donated to The Hall.

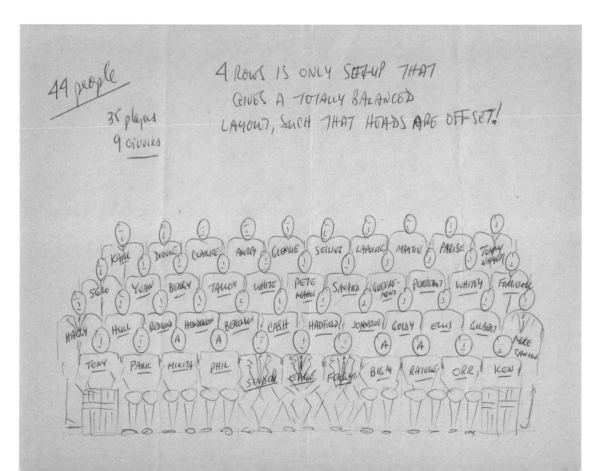

A historic moment in time is captured in three mediums: The official portrait of Team Canada '72 is shown at the top, which had been preceded by a drawing of how the photographer envisioned the seating arrangement and a screen shot from Al Stewart that shows the players assembling for the portrait.

At a press conference following the game, Gretzky stated, "If the Hockey Hall of Fame wants my uniform, then it's the only place it will go." As he slowly undressed, each piece of equipment was tossed into his equipment bag, zipped up for the final time and handed to Colin Campbell, who had been a teammate with the Edmonton Oilers during the 1979-80 season and was working for the NHL at the time. Campbell gave the bag to his brother Cam, who delivered the equipment untouched to The Hall. Included were his jersey, helmet, Nike 'Zoom Air' skates, pants, socks, gloves, shoulder pads, elbow pads, shin pads, jock strap, garter belt and the Rangers' equipment bag in which they were carried. He later added the stick and puck he used to tally his final NHL point.

"My last game in New York was my greatest day in hockey," Gretzky told journalist Scott Morrison. "Everything you enjoy about the sport of hockey as a kid, driving to the game with mom and dad, looking in the stands and seeing your mom and dad and your friends — that all came together in that last game in New York."

Priceless.

THE BRAND

A Hands-On Approach to Marketing

While in its earliest years, The Hall may have been perceived as a venerable institution, proudly, if conservatively, guarding the legacy of the game, the modern era — especially since the move downtown — sees it on the cutting edge of marketing and communications, helping it expand its fan base and grow its brand worldwide.

"Is the Hockey Hall of Fame only for those who excelled at the highest level?" asks Peter Jagla, vice-president of marketing and attraction services, rhetorically. "No, everybody is a cast member in hockey. We recognize that we have to continue to diversify in what we offer and how we attract new fans wherever they are, no matter if they played the game or not."

Spurred by market research, The Hall initiated a youth campaign promoting itself as an interactive attraction. Once inside, instead of a "typical" museum with roped-off displays of artifacts from bygone eras, visitors find a modern facility offering hands-on experiences enhanced by the latest technologies. The progressive approach includes a complete update of every square inch of The Hall every few years with the exception of the Canadiens replica dressing room from the old Montreal Forum — some things you just don't touch — ensuring the exhibits remain fresh and exciting.

It works. The Hall has become a pilgrimage destination for fans of all ages. They come to touch the exhibits, take 'selfies' with the Stanley Cup and generally immerse themselves in the hockey experience.

Inside the NHLPA Game Time attraction, for example, fans line up to try their luck against 'virtual' NHL talent in state-of-the-art, interactive games on a model rink. 'Shut Out' offers an opportunity to play goalie by grabbing a glove and blocker and facing shots from video images of superstars such as Sidney Crosby, Connor McDavid and Alexander Ovechkin, who fire weighted sponge pucks at speeds up to 70 mph through openings in an 8-by-10-foot video screen that features simulated game action. 'Shoot Out' puts the stick and pucks in the hands of the shooter, pitting them against

life-sized, computer-simulated versions of the likes of Carey Price and Henrik Lundqvist. Censors process the trajectory and speed of each shot, prompting the goalie to move and make the save. It's not so easy; just ask Wayne Gretzky. (*Please see page 79.*) Each simulation game is recorded on a video system that allows fans to share their best shots (or saves) on social media.

"Playing the game at The Hall has an aura of glory; the glory of youth or combining the love of the game with legends," explains Jagla. "Sport is something to have fun with, but it also brings out the competitive nature of visitors."

The hands-on approach has been so widely embraced by The Hall that it continues to be featured in marketing campaigns. In 2017, a good-natured commercial poked fun at the world of virtual reality. Entitled 'Real Reality,' the spots invited fans, especially millennials, to visit The Hall and see — and touch — for themselves "Where Virtual Reality ends, Real Reality begins!" As the voice-over suggests, "When you're looking at Sidney Crosby's gloves, you're looking at Sidney Crosby's gloves!" The Hall even distributed goggles – made from the "highest grade of generic cardboard," laughs Jagla — as part of the fun with the campaign. Along with TV spots, the commercial ran at key cinemas across Canada before feature films and on scoreboards in NHL arenas.

The Hall was also behind the production of *Stanley's Game Seven*, the first hockey movie produced in 3D. The film pushes the boundaries of 3D filmmaking in the sports genre to groundbreaking levels, while delivering on The Hall's promise of offering visitors a unique hockey experience. The realism of

A young visitor attempts to
stop a virtual shooter in The
Hall's Interactive Area.

The replica home dressing room from the fabled Forum in Montreal is the only exhibit that has not been changed since The Hall's 1993 opening. Canadiens alumni have sat in their former spots, reminiscing about the amazing days gone by.

H. RICHARD
H. BACKSTROM
G. TREMBLAY
J.C. TREMBLAY
R. ROUSSEAU
T. HARPER
J. FERGUSON
C. LAROSE
T. HARRIS
Y. COURNOYER
N. PRICE
R. VACHON
L. ROCHEFORT
J. FERGUSON
J. LAPERRIERE
L. AUBUT
Geoffrion, Bernie #5
Moore, Dickie #12
5
5
12
12
2

the live-action sequences was achieved using a custom-built rail system laid over an actual ice surface that helped propel high-speed cameras at speeds up to 130 kilometres per second.

Stanley's Game Seven introduces a group of young men who gather at the local small-town rink for their once-a-week hockey game, the highlight of their lives, following them as they compete in their very own game seven. Among the classic playoff moments featured are signature plays of Hall-of-Famers Bobby Orr, Wayne Gretzky and Mario Lemieux.

The movie was produced by Network Entertainment, which had previously partnered with The Hall on a number of successful ventures, including the Gemini Award-winning Legends of Hockey series and the *Stanley Cup Odyssey* film.

Stanley's Game Seven repeats several times a day in The Hall's TSN Theatre.

Beyond self-generated marketing initiatives, The Hall also plays a key role — thanks to its extensive collection and its dynamic facility — in helping other organizations celebrate milestones and anniversaries. In recent years, it hosted exhibits on the centennials of the Montreal Canadiens, Toronto Maple Leafs and the NHL itself, as well as the 125th anniversary of the Stanley Cup. In 1999, it did a terrific job on the Wayne Gretzky exhibit, which was supplemented by items donated by the superstar's father, Walter. It also turned the Olympic good fortune of Canada's men's and women's team over the years into increased ticket sales, the 'Lucky Loonie' exhibit from Salt Lake City in 2002 and the 'Golden Goal' display of Sidney Crosby's winner in Vancouver in 2010 being among the most popular attractions.

The Hall benefits from one of the oldest adages in marketing, 'Location, location, location,' thanks to its downtown, and beautiful, Toronto home. Consistently among the city's top tourist draws, it takes advantage of attendance spikes whenever Original Six teams (Boston, Chicago, Detroit, Montreal and New York), as well as the Pennsylvania franchises, Philadelphia and Pittsburgh, are in town to face the Leafs. Similar jumps occur when Major League Baseball teams from those U.S. markets visit the Blue Jays. (Team colours of visiting fans at The Hall's Spirit of Hockey retail store are usually a good hint as to who's in town on any given day.) Traditionally, The Hall draws on average 65 percent of its attendance from Canada, 25 percent from the United States and 10 percent from overseas.

Original game-action footage was filmed over a two-week period to increase the impact of *Stanley's Game Seven*.

The Hall is home to some of the most dramatic monuments in the hockey world, both inside the museum and out.

'Our Game' is an homage to Canada's love for hockey. The bronze maquette was created by Edie Parker of Oakville, Ontario, to coincide with the grand opening of the Great Hall in 1993. The sculpture, 17 feet in length and six-and-a-half-feet tall, was inspired by a 1970s magazine ad and depicts five excited young-sters clinging to the boards during a hockey game. Its location is at the Front Street entrance to The Hall and invites fans to take photos while standing between the bronze players.

Just east of 'Our Game' is a tribute to Team Canada '72. While The Hall inducts individuals and not teams, this monument commemorates the achievement of the Canadian team that faced the Soviet Union's best hockey players in an eight-game tournament in September 1972. With the series tied going into Game 8 in Moscow, Paul Henderson scored with just 34 seconds remaining in that deciding game to give Canada the victory, a defining moment in Canadian sports history. The Royal Canadian Mint sponsored the Team Canada '72 Millennium Tribute monument, which was officially unveiled on a small strip of land just outside the Great Hall on November 10, 2000, with all but two of the team members present for the ceremony. It now stands in perpetuity for the thousands of pedestrians who pass the busy corner to see.

Within The Hall itself stand two giant sentries, watching over guests. One is Cyclone Taylor, one of hockey's first superstars, and who later in life served on The Hall's Selection Committee. The other is Ken Dryden, standing regally as he leans on his goalie stick, a pose he struck on hundreds of occasions while the puck was in the opposing end of the rink during his years starring with the Montreal Canadiens.

On November 5, 2010, Honoured Members Johnny Bower and Billy Smith, both goaltenders, were joined by Pat Quinn to unveil 'At The Crease,' a larger-than-life statue honouring Ken Danby's iconic painting of the same name. The statue "guards" the Spirit of Hockey retail store entrance facing Sam Pollock Square within Brookfield Place, and is another extremely popular photo opportunity for fans.

On June 10, 2016, the hockey world lost one of its greatest players and ambassadors when Gordie Howe passed away. To honour his memory, a statue almost eight feet in height was unveiled of 'Mr. Hockey' at the entrance to The Hall on March 10, 2017. Howe's sons Mark and Marty participated in the unveiling, joined by Hall Chairman Lanny McDonald. The statue stands larger than life, just like Howe's legend, welcoming visitors.

If there is an area of confusion with the brand, it has to do with the common misconception that The Hall is the 'NHL Hall of Fame.' Certainly, the majority of the inductees are drawn from the league's talent pool and The Hall acknowledges the contributions of the NHL both on and off the ice through the years, but as Bill Hay, chairman, stated in 2003, "The Hockey Hall of Fame is a separate and distinct incorporated entity with a board of directors operating independently of the NHL or any other third party."

The Hall proudly showcases the depth and breadth of the game, including women's hockey, international competitions, junior, minor pro, university, sledge hockey, deaf hockey and just about any other version of the game wherever it is played. The international component, in fact, has been key to its brand expansion specifically through a partnership with the International Ice Hockey Federation (IIHF), which led to the opening of the 3,500-square-foot World of Hockey Zone in 1998, dedicated to the global game. It features displays on Olympics, World Cup and many other tournaments, profiles of all 75 IIHF member countries as well as the IIHF Honour Roll exhibit, which pays tribute to the finest players and executives from around the world.

Among those honoured in The Hall for their exceptional international careers are Anatoli Tarasov, the Soviet coach inducted as a Builder in 1974, Players Valeri Kharlamov (inducted in 2005) and Vladislav Tretiak (1989), neither of whom played in the NHL. Viacheslav Fetisov (2001), Igor Larionov (2008) and Sergei Makarov (2016) starred in the Soviet Union/Russia for several years before finishing their careers in the NHL.

Another important step forward was admission of women beginning in 2010 in the same Player Category alongside their male counterparts. Since Cammi Granato and Angela James were elected that year, The Hall has elected Geraldine Heaney (2013), Angela Ruggiero (2015) and Danielle Goyette (2017), all pioneers of the quickly-growing women's game.

The Hall has had a few fun and very successful TV commercials and campaigns over the years — including several award-winners.

'SO MUCH FUN, YOU WON'T KNOW WHAT HIT YA!' | 1997

The Hall's VP of Marketing Bryan Black contracted agency Pirate Radio and Television to deliver the message that The Hall was a fun place. The agency's Terry O'Reilly developed the concept for a 30-second commercial. "The idea showed a man walking up to an interactive machine, pushing a button, and being pelted in the face with pucks — to his utter shock. The man smiles and a voiceover then says, 'The Hockey Hall of a Fame. So much fun, you won't know what hit ya!'" The Hall had never before done a television campaign, and spending thousands of dollars on TV was risky. Eventually, Hall chairman Scotty Morrison gave his stamp of approval to the concept. Everyone held their breath.

Toronto-based actor David Huband was hired, and a fictitious interactive Johnny Bower exhibit was chosen as the setting. "During the filming, the director would stand beside the camera with a bucket of (sponge) rubber pucks, and just threw them at my face," chuckled Huband. "My head started to hurt after a couple of hours, but I stayed with it until the bitter end." His expressions were priceless, especially when his glasses were knocked askew, and the tagline captured the essence of the new Hall.

"It was not the typical hockey commercial, however, the results were incredible," stated Black. "Attendance went way up."

The commercial won at the Bessie Awards (honouring Canadian television advertising) that year for best performance (Huband) and also earned a distinguished honour for The Hall for best Canadian Commercial of the Year produced for less than $50,000. It also set the tone for other successful Hall commercials to come.

'WHITE GLOVES' | 2008

The 'White Gloves' campaign showed Phil Pritchard, the Keeper of the Cup, doing everyday activities while wearing the white gloves he is so well known for when carrying the Stanley Cup. The humourous commercial reinforced The Hall as the home of hockey's most important artifact, where visitors can actually touch, kiss or hug the Cup.

'DO IT ALL AT THE HALL'

This popular campaign, starting in 2006, helps portray The Hall in a modern light, using vivid colours and debunking taboos of a standard museum. It shows visitors playing, yelling, eating and embracing the Cup — very un-museum-like.

SUCCESS

'MOST HOCKEY DREAMS DIE' | 2011

'GAMETIME' | 2014 & 2015

Taxi Canada was the advertising agency behind The Hall's 2011 campaign, 'Most Hockey Dreams Die,' a four-commercial parody with realistic footage and brilliant copywriting. The commercials were filmed at George Bell Arena in Toronto, also incorporating archival footage and instructional videos from Hockey Canada. L. Harvey Gold, whose unique and authoritative voice had been used earlier on The Hall's licensed and award-winning 'Legends of Hockey' television series, stated: "Most hockey dreams die. Come see the ones that didn't... at the Hockey Hall of Fame."

Each commercial channels the derailment of a hockey career: finding another passion (a love interest); limitations of a skill set (can't shoot); an injury (an awkward split save); and the impact of the invention of the flavoured potato chip (for someone lacking willpower).

The campaign cleaned up at the Bessie Awards, with one taking the 2012 International Award at the Cannes Lions, the world's leading competition for the creative and marketing communications industry.

The Gametime 'Shut Out' and 'Shoot Out' commercials used actors and, for the first time, current NHL players, in a make-believe audition for roles in The Hall's interactive games. In these humourous commercials, several candidates naïvely believe they are Hall-worthy. Inevitably, an NHLer emerges as the best of the competition: Corey Perry of the Anaheim Ducks for the 'Shoot Out' role and Jonathan Bernier, then of the Toronto Maple Leafs, for the 'Shut Out' role.

It's not all open ice when it comes to marketing The Hall. Like other attractions, it faces its share of challenges, including increased competition for entertainment dollars, tourism disruptions caused by world events and economic downturns, and labour disputes like NHL player strikes. Each can take its toll, and has, on the not-for-profit institution. However, its brand is strong and with a focus on reinvesting in capital improvements, exhibits and the preservation of artifacts, its game plan is smart. The Hall consistently ranks as a top attraction in Toronto, and it has successfully expanded its relationship within the community through mutually-beneficial sponsorships and partnerships.

"The Hall of Fame relies on multiple revenue streams, including admissions, sponsorships, inductions, hospitality, outreach, retail, photo licensing and consulting other hockey museums in order to maintain its spot as the premier hockey attraction in the world," explains Jagla. "If you rely on revenue from admissions alone, you're holding yourself vulnerable to the environment of external forces. We like to skate with our heads up."

It's all part of the brand.

The awe-inspiring Great Hall is housed in the former bank building, and features the plaques of the Honoured Members, the NHL merit trophies and, in its place of honour, the Stanley Cup.

A HALL FOR ALL

Growing the Hockey Community

You have to hand it to Captain James T. Sutherland. When he first started thinking about a hall of fame to honour hockey's greats in the early 1940s, he had no building, no backing and, ultimately, no host city. But he did have a dream, and, as it turned out, that was plenty.

Today, thanks in large part to the good captain's perseverance, not only does the Hockey Hall of Fame find itself in an iconic home in downtown Toronto, but enjoying wide support as a world-class sports hall and museum in which Honoured Member status has come to represent the ultimate career achievement for the legends of the game. Perhaps more importantly, The Hall is where dreams are spawned, and just as Sutherland discovered, there's no telling where that might lead.

From the start of inductions in 1945, when nine Players and two Builders were inducted into its first class and announced through a small item in the newspaper, The Hall now counts 276 Honoured Members in the Player Category, 107 in the Builder Category, and another 16 in the Referee/Linesman Category. Inductions have become an international-level event, preceded by a weekend of celebrations and followed by a formal ceremony attended by thousands in the incredible Allen Lambert Galleria at Brookfield Place, with countless more watching on television and following through social media.

The Hall first found a home in a shared facility, and then with the assistance of the National Hockey League and the City of Toronto, a beautiful location was built on the grounds of the Canadian National Exhibition. In 1993, the vision was further developed, with the move to an extraordinary heritage bank building — itself worth the price of admission. Inside, an embarrassment of hockey riches would grow to include an expansive collection that dates back more than a century in some cases, as well as interactive exhibits that are state-of-the-art. And then there's the *ne plus ultra* of professional sports trophies, the Stanley Cup, which calls The Hall home.

"The vision from the outset is to continually enhance the attraction and introduce timely new features that tell the story of hockey as the game evolves," states Jeff Denomme, the president and CEO of the Hockey Hall of Fame. "The sum of all its parts, a complementary mix of traditional, theatrical and interactive exhibit presentations, focused on past and current events, is what makes The Hall such a highly-rated and immersive guest experience."

The Hall is a self-sufficient operation, and as a non-profit organization, reinvests surplus funds to constantly attract new and repeat visitors. It is recognized internationally as a model for innovation and efficiency among sport halls of fame and museums. Sprawled across 90,000 square feet (once exhibition spaces, the Resource Centre and offices are factored in), it has grown exponentially over the years due to its success as an attraction and its status as a multi-faceted resource serving all of hockey.

"Ultimately, we have to ensure The Hall remains accessible and continues to deliver on its high value ratings from casual to hardcore hockey fans," says Denomme. "Admissions are only part of the equation. Sponsorships, hospitality events, outreach programs, licensing partnerships, consultancy services and particularly the Spirit of Hockey retail store have all proven to be highly successful revenue generators. This not only helps sustain our financial autonomy, but also allows us to re-invest in the fan experience."

In 2017, a special Tim Hortons opened in Brookfield Place adjacent to The Hall's Spirit of Hockey store. The location is the only one licensed to include artifacts from The Hall.

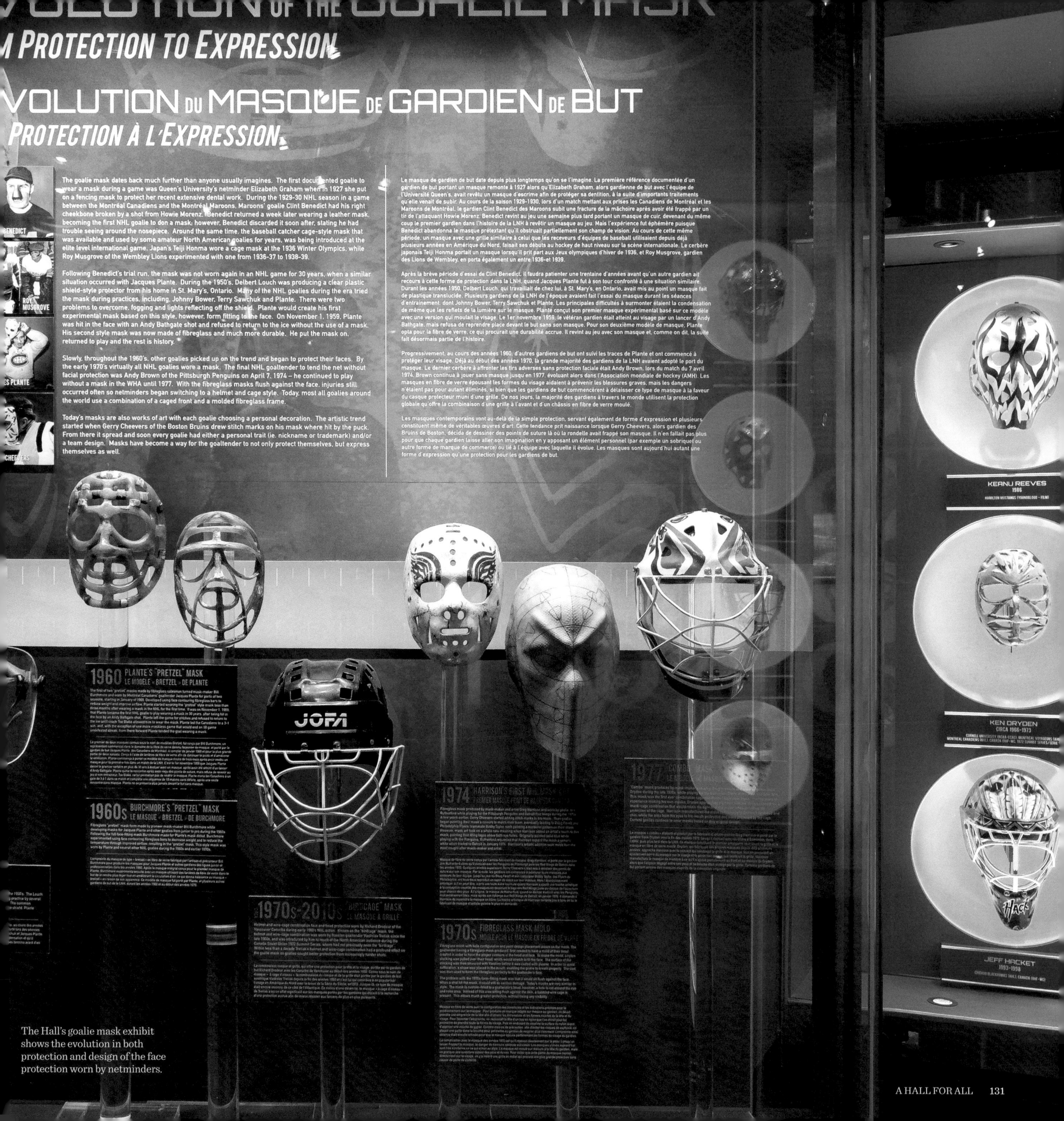

VOLUTION DU MASQUE DE GARDIEN DE BUT
PROTECTION À L'EXPRESSION

The goalie mask dates back much further than anyone usually imagines. The first documented goalie to wear a mask during a game was Queen's University's netminder Elizabeth Graham when in 1927 she put on a fencing mask to protect her recent extensive dental work. During the 1929-30 NHL season in a game between the Montréal Canadiens and the Montréal Maroons, Maroons' goalie Clint Benedict had his right cheekbone broken by a shot from Howie Morenz. Benedict returned a week later wearing a leather mask, becoming the first NHL goalie to don a mask; however, Benedict discarded it soon after, stating he had trouble seeing around the nosepiece. Around the same time, the baseball catcher cage-style mask that was available and used by some amateur North American goalies for years, was being introduced at the elite level international game. Japan's Teiji Honma wore a cage mask at the 1936 Winter Olympics, while Roy Musgrove of the Wembley Lions experimented with one from 1936-37 to 1938-39.

Following Benedict's trial run, the mask was not worn again in an NHL game for 30 years, when a similar situation occurred with Jacques Plante. During the 1950's, Delbert Louch was producing a clear plastic shield-style protector from his home in St. Mary's, Ontario. Many of the NHL goalies during the era tried the mask during practices, including, Johnny Bower, Terry Sawchuk and Plante. There were two problems to overcome, fogging and lights reflecting off the shield. Plante would create his first experimental mask based on this style, however, form fitting to the face. On November 1, 1959, Plante was hit in the face with an Andy Bathgate shot and refused to return to the ice without the use of a mask. His second style mask was now made of fibreglass and much more durable. He put the mask on, returned to play and the rest is history.

Slowly, throughout the 1960's, other goalies picked up on the trend and began to protect their faces. By the early 1970's virtually all NHL goalies wore a mask. The final NHL goaltender to tend the net without facial protection was Andy Brown of the Pittsburgh Penguins on April 7, 1974 – he continued to play without a mask in the WHA until 1977. With the fibreglass masks flush against the face, injuries still occurred often so netminders began switching to a helmet and cage style. Today, most all goalies around the world use a combination of a caged front and a molded fibreglass frame.

Today's masks are also works of art with each goalie choosing a personal decoration. The artistic trend started when Gerry Cheevers of the Boston Bruins drew stitch marks on his mask where hit by the puck. From there it spread and soon every goalie had either a personal trait (ie. nickname or trademark) and/or a team design. Masks have become a way for the goaltender to not only protect themselves, but express themselves as well.

Le masque de gardien de but date depuis plus longtemps qu'on se l'imagine. La première référence documentée d'un gardien de but portant un masque remonte à 1927 alors qu'Elizabeth Graham, alors gardienne de but avec l'équipe de l'Université Queen's, avait revêtu un masque d'escrime afin de protéger sa dentition, à la suite d'importants traitements qu'elle venait de subir. Au cours de la saison 1929-1930, lors d'un match mettant aux prises les Canadiens de Montréal et les Maroons de Montréal, le gardien Clint Benedict des Maroons subit une fracture de la mâchoire après avoir été frappé par un tir de l'attaquant Howie Morenz. Benedict revint au jeu une semaine plus tard portant un masque de cuir, devenant du même coup le premier gardien dans l'histoire de la LNH à revêtir un masque au jeu. Mais l'expérience fut éphémère puisque Benedict abandonna le masque prétextant qu'il obstruait partiellement son champ de vision. Au cours de cette même période, un masque avec une grille similaire à celui que les receveurs d'équipes de baseball utilisent depuis déjà plusieurs années en Amérique du Nord, faisait ses débuts au hockey de haut niveau sur la scène internationale. Le cerbère japonais Teiji Honma portait un masque lorsqu'il prit part aux Jeux olympiques d'hiver de 1936, et Roy Musgrove, gardien des Lions de Wembley, en porta également un entre 1936-et 1939.

Après la brève période d'essai de Clint Benedict, il faudra patienter une trentaine d'années avant qu'un autre gardien ait recours à cette forme de protection dans la LNH, quand Jacques Plante fut à son tour confronté à une situation similaire. Durant les années 1950, Delbert Louch, qui travaillait de chez lui, à St. Mary's, en Ontario, avait mis au point un masque fait de plastique translucide. Plusieurs gardiens de la LNH de l'époque avaient fait l'essai du masque durant les séances d'entraînement, dont Johnny Bower, Terry Sawchuk et Plante. Les principales difficultés à surmonter étaient la condensation de même que les reflets de la lumière sur le masque. Plante conçut son premier masque expérimental basé sur ce modèle avec une version qui moulait le visage. Le 1er novembre 1959, le vétéran gardien était atteint au visage par un lancer d'Andy Bathgate, mais refusa de reprendre place devant le but sans son masque. Pour son deuxième modèle de masque, Plante opta pour la fibre de verre, ce qui procurait une durabilité accrue. Il revint au jeu avec son masque et, comme on dit, la suite fait désormais partie de l'histoire

Progressivement, au cours des années 1960, d'autres gardiens de but ont suivi les traces de Plante et ont commencé à protéger leur visage. Déjà au début des années 1970, la grande majorité des gardiens de la LNH avaient adopté le port du masque. Le dernier cerbère à affronter les tirs adverses sans protection faciale était Andy Brown, lors du match du 7 avril 1974. Brown continua à jouer sans masque jusqu'en 1977, évoluant alors dans l'Association mondiale de hockey (AMH). Les masques en fibre de verre épousant les formes du visage aidaient à prévenir les blessures graves, mais les dangers n'étaient pas pour autant éliminés, si bien que les gardiens de but commencèrent à délaisser ce type de masque à la faveur du casque protecteur muni d'une grille. De nos jours, la majorité des gardiens à travers le monde utilisent la protection globale qu'offre la combinaison d'une grille à l'avant et d'un châssis en fibre de verre moulé.

Les masques contemporains vont au-delà de la simple protection, servant également de forme d'expression et plusieurs constituent même de véritables œuvres d'art. Cette tendance prit naissance lorsque Gerry Cheevers, alors gardien des Bruins de Boston, décida de dessiner des points de suture là où la rondelle avait frappé son masque. Il n'en fallait pas plus pour que chaque gardien laisse aller son imagination en y apposant un élément personnel (par exemple un sobriquet ou autre forme de marque de commerce) ou lié à l'équipe avec laquelle il évolue. Les masques sont aujourd'hui autant une forme d'expression qu'une protection pour les gardiens de but.

KEANU REEVES 1986
HAMILTON MUSTANGS (YOUNGBLOOD - FILM)

KEN DRYDEN
CIRCA 1966-1973
CORNELL UNIVERSITY (NCAA-ECAC) MONTREAL VOYAGEURS (AHL)
MONTREAL CANADIENS (NHL), CANADA (NAT'L), 1972 SUMMIT SERIES / SÉRIE

1960 PLANTE'S "PRETZEL" MASK
LE MODÈLE « BRETZEL » DE PLANTE

The first of two "pretzel" masks made by fibreglass salesman turned mask-maker Bill Burchmore and worn by Montréal Canadiens' goaltender Jacques Plante for parts of two seasons, starting in January of 1960. Developed using face contouring fibreglass bars to reduce weight and improve airflow. Plante started wearing the "pretzel" style mask less than three months after wearing a mask in the NHL for the first time. It was on November 1, 1959, that Plante became the first NHL goalie to play wearing a mask in 35 years, after being hit in the face by an Andy Bathgate shot. Plante left the game for protection and refused to return to the ice until coach Toe Blake allowed him to wear the mask. Plante led the Canadiens to a 3-1 win, and, with the exception of one more maskless game that would end an 18 game undefeated streak, from there forward Plante tended the goal wearing a mask.

Le premier de deux masques conçus sous le nom de modèles Bretzel, fut conçu par Bill Burchmore, un représentant commercial dans le domaine de la fibre de verre devenu façonneur de masque, et porté par le gardien de but Jacques Plante, des Canadiens de Montréal, à compter de janvier 1960 et pour la plupart de deux saisons. Conçu à l'aide de lanières de fibre de verre afin de diminuer le poids et d'améliorer la ventilation. Plante commença à porter ce modèle de masque moins de trois mois après avoir rendu un masque pour la première fois dans un match de la LNH. C'est le 1er novembre 1959 que Jacques Plante devint le gardien cerbère le plus de 35 ans à évoluer avec un masque, après avoir été atteint au visage par un lancer d'Andy Bathgate. Plante quitta la rencontre après avoir reçu des points de suture, mais refusa de revenir au jeu si non entraîneur Toe Blake, ne lui permettait pas de revêtir le masque. Plante mena les Canadiens à un gain de 3 à 1 dans ce match et compléta une séquence de 18 matchs sans défaite, après une seule rencontre sans masque. Plante ne présenta plus jamais devant le but sans masque.

1960s BURCHMORE'S "PRETZEL" MASK
LE MASQUE « BRETZEL » DE BURCHMORE

Fibreglass "pretzel" mask form made by pioneer mask-maker Bill Burchmore while developing masks for Jacques Plante and other goalies from junior to pro during the 1960s. Following the full face-fitting mask Burchmore made for Plante's mask during practice, Burchmore experimented using face contouring fibreglass bars to decrease weight and to reduce the temperature through improved airflow, resulting in the "pretzel" mask. This style mask was worn by Plante and several other NHL goalies during the 1960s and earlier 1970s.

La forme de masque de type « bretzel » en fibre de verre fabriqué par l'artisan et précurseur Bill Burchmore pour produire les masques pour Jacques Plante et autres gardiens évoluant tant au niveau junior et professionnel dans les années 1960. Après le masque intégral conçu pour le premier masque de Plante, Burchmore expérimenta ensuite avec un masque utilisant des lanières de fibre de verre épousant les formes du visage afin de réduire le poids et la température à travers une ventilation supérieure, ce qui résulta en ce qui se nomme le masque « bretzel » Ce modèle de masque fut porté par Plante, et plusieurs autres gardiens de but de la LNH, durant les années 1960 au au début des années 1970.

JOFA

1970s-2010s "BIRDCAGE" MASK LE MASQUE À GRILLE

Helmet and wire-cage combination face and head protection worn by Richard Brodeur of the Vancouver Canucks during early 1980s NHL action. Known as the "birdcage" mask, the helmet and wire-cage combination was worn by Russian goaltender Vladislav Tretiak since the late 1960s, and was introduced by him to much of the North American audience during the Canada-Soviet Union 1972 Summit Series, where had not previously worn the "birdcage" Within less than a decade Tretiak's helmet and wire-cage combination had a profound effect on the goalie mask as goalies sought better protection from increasingly harder shots.

La combinaison casque et grille, qui offre une protection pour la tête et le visage, portée par le gardien but Richard Brodeur avec les Canucks de Vancouver au début des années 1980. Connu sous le nom de masque « à cage d'oiseau » la combinaison du casque et de la grille était portée par le gardien de but soviétique Vladislav Tretiak depuis la fin des années 1960 et ce fut lui qui en fit connaître à un population d'usage en Amérique du Nord avant la tenue de la Série du siècle en 1972. Jusque-là, ce type de masque était encore inconnu de ce côté de l'Atlantique. En moins d'une décennie, le modèle « à cage d'oiseau » de Tretiak a eu un effet significatif sur les masques porté par les gardiens de but qui désiraient une meilleure protection devant des lancers de plus en plus puissant.

1974 HARRISON'S FIRST NHL MASK
PREMIER MASQUE DE LA LNH D'HARRISON

Fibreglass mask produced by mask-maker and artist Greg Harrison and worn by goalie in Rutherford while playing for the Pittsburgh Penguins and Detroit Red Wings during the 1970s era junior action. Greg Cheevers started putting stitch marks in his mask. Years later he began painting their mask's concepts to match their team, eventually backing to Billy Smith and Philadelphia Flyers teammate Bobby Taylor, each painting a workhorse goalie on their mask. However, mask, art took on a whole new meaning when Harrison being on an artist's touch to the mask, painting this thing logos above both eye holes. Originally painted blue when playing with the Penguins, Rutherford requested that Harrison support the mask a greenery white when traded to Detroit in January 1976. Harrison's artistic addition soon made him the most sought after masks maker and artist.

Masque de fibre de verre conçu par l'artiste-façonneur Greg Harrison, et porté par le gardien Jim Rutherford alors qu'il évoluait avec les Penguins de Pittsburgh et les Red Wings de Detroit dans les années 1970. Quelques années auparavant, Gerry Cheevers s'était mis à dessiner des points de suture à même son masque. Plus tard, les gardiens ont commencé à peinturer leurs masques afin de refléter leur équipe. Puis au début, Billy Smith et son coéquipier chez les Flyers de Philadelphie, Bobby Taylor, arboraient chacun un cheval de course sur leur masque. Mais l'art atteindrait atteignait un tout autre stade, lorsque Harrison ajouta une touche d'artiste à même un masque, en y peinturant les logos de son équipe au-dessus des deux ouvertures pour les yeux. Au départ, il arbora un logo bleu lorsque porté par le gardien chez les Penguins de Pittsburgh, mais à sa demande d'Harrison, lorsqu'il fut échangé chez les Red Wings de Detroit en janvier 1976, il demanda à Harrison de repeindre le masque en blanc. La touche artistique de Harrison lui mérita le titre le plus en demande en tant que façonneur de masque et de véritable œuvre d'art la plus en demande.

1970s FIBREGLASS MASK MOLD
MOULE POUR LE MASQUE EN FIBRE DE VERRE

Fibreglass mask with hole configuration and paint design placement shown on the mold. The goaltender having a fibreglass mask produced first needed to have a mold of their head created in order to have the proper contours of the head and face. To make the mold, a nylon stocking was pulled over their head, which would smooth to fit the face. The surface of this stocking was then dressed with liquid plaster, which was coated with plaster. In order to avoid suffocation, a straw was placed in the mouth, enabling the goalie to breath properly. The cast was then used to form the fibreglass perfectly to the goaltender's face.

The problem with the 1970s form-fitting mask was that it would sit flush against the face. When a shot hit the mask, it would still re-section damage. Today's masks are very similar in style. The main difference comes from the cage mask in front which wraps around the eye and nose area. Instead of this area sitting flush against the skin, a bubble wire cage is present. This allows much greater protection, without hindering vision.

Masque en fibre de verre sur lequel la configuration des trous et des emplacements prévus pour la peinture sont ici envisagés. Pour produire un masque adapté aux mesures précises, on devait d'abord prévoir une empreinte de la tête afin d'obtenir les dimensions et les formes exactes de la tête et du visage. Pour façonner l'empreinte, on recouvrait la tête d'un bas en nylon que l'on étirait pour bien épouser les formes du visage. Puis on endossait du plâtre liquide sur la surface du bas en nylon qui s'épousait une couche de plâtre. Comme mesure de précaution, afin d'éviter les risques de suffocation, on plaçait une paille dans la bouche afin qu'il puisse respirer librement. Ensuite, ce moule étroit qui épousait les formes du visage permettait de parfaitement les contours du masque du gardien. La combinaison masque de type bretzel des années 1970 sur lui reposait directement sur le visage, ce qui, lorsqu'un tir atteignait la grille, on notait une protection accrue, sans nuire à la vision du gardien.

1977 COMBO MASK
LE MASQUE COMBI

"Combo" mask produced by mask-maker Greg Harrison during the late 1970s, while employing both a cage and fibreglass frame. This mask was the first ever combination mask experimenting make both. Harrison approached the mask-cage combination that would enable the goalie to utilize protection of the cage. Harrison experimented the area of the chin, while the extra hole that it's area to his mask production and the continuing Cornell Goalies continue to wear masks based on this original design.

JEFF HACKETT
1993-1998
CHICAGO BLACKHAWKS (NHL), CANADA (NAT'L-WC)

La combinaison « combi » étudiait et produit par le fabricant et artisan-façonneur Greg Harrison à partir du gardien Brian Hayward de la LNH. Ce masque a était fabriqué le premier et proposant à produire une combinaison masque et grille. Parce que plusieurs de ses clients ont travaillé sur le visage en fibre de verre du masque. Harrison opta pour la grille et pour le rebord de la fibre de verre fibre de verre moulé. Réalisée par la protection offerte par la grille, une protection plus accrue à la région du menton. Dans des masques que les gardiens de Cornell continuent de porter, ce modèle de Harrison inspiré par avec son cru de série protection pour la partie inférieure du visage, et des idées de l'artisan Greg Harrison allons ce qui n'allait conçu en son de la poursuivre continuité.

The Hall's goalie mask exhibit shows the evolution in both protection and design of the face protection worn by netminders.

The Hall's 75th anniversary in 2018 provided the perfect opportunity to give a nod to the leadership over the years, each of whom helped grow The Hall and pave the way towards the historic milestone and also those who will guide it forward.

BOBBY HEWITSON (left)

After retiring from refereeing at the end of the 1933-34 NHL season, Hewitson was recruited to join the newly-conceived 'Hot Stove League' radio show to discuss hockey matters during intermissions of Toronto Maple Leafs home games. He was a member of the committee that established Canada's Sports Hall of Fame in 1955, and joined the museum as its first curator in 1957. When it was decided that the Hockey Hall of Fame would be located in Toronto, Hewitson assumed the role of curator in addition to his responsibilities with Canada's sports hall. Hewitson played an integral role in the development of The Hall, and was inducted as a Builder in 1963. He retired in 1967 and passed away early in 1969.

MAURICE 'LEFTY' REID (right)

In 1967, Reid was hired to assist Hewitson at both Canada's Sports Hall of Fame and the Hockey Hall of Fame, housed in the same building. He was named curator of the Hockey Hall of Fame in 1968 and immediately set out to raise its profile, starting with re-writing the biographies of Honoured Members and creating a library of books and newspaper clippings. He also sought out artifacts and photo collections. Reid would write basic policies for conservation, research, library and exhibits, none of which had existed. His most public role saw him delivering the Stanley Cup to champions for 18 years, packing it and driving it himself. He was curator at The Hall until 1992. Reid was instrumental in establishing the Canadian Association of Sports Heritage (CASH) and the International Sports Heritage Association (ISHA). He received ISHA's distinguished service award in 1988.

IAN 'SCOTTY' MORRISON (left)

In 1954, at 24 years of age, Morrison became the NHL's youngest referee at that time. He would become the league's referee-in-chief in 1965. In 1985, he was named the NHL's vice-president, officiating. NHL President John Ziegler appointed him vice-president, project development and president, Hockey Hall of Fame in 1986. He was named chairman and chief executive officer in 1991. Morrison is widely credited for providing the vision and creativity behind The Hall's new downtown location, including building a team that would oversee the renovation and development of the site. He officially retired as chairman of the board of directors in 1998, but remains on the board. He was elected as an Honoured Member in the Builder Category in 1999, and was named one of two Stanley Cup trustees in 2002.

DAVID TAYLOR (right)

Taylor was recruited from the Corporation of Massey Hall and Roy Thomson Hall in May 1991 to help oversee the move of The Hall from the CNE Grounds to its current home. As president of The Hall, he led the design, management and staff teams to produce the new 'world standard' Hockey Hall of Fame. He was also instrumental in bringing in new corporate sponsors to assist with funding the capital costs of building and equipping the new facilities. Besides his leadership role in successfully launching The Hall at its new location, including major events to welcome and showcase The Hall to its Honoured Members and other key constituents, Taylor's experience with corporate hospitality events helped introduce an important revenue stream to The Hall.

BILL HAY *(left)*

Hay won the Calder Trophy as the league's top rookie with Chicago in 1959-60, and the Stanley Cup in 1961. He retired following the 1966-67 season, and went on to a career in the oil industry. In 1991, he was named president & CEO of the Calgary Flames, and later served as president and COO of Hockey Canada. Hay led the negotiations to merge Hockey Canada and the Canadian Amateur Hockey Association into the Canadian Hockey Association (Hockey Canada). He sat on The Hall's Selection Committee from 1980 until 1997, and served on the board of directors from 1995 until 2013, 15 years as chair. Under his leadership, The Hall strengthened relations with key partners, including the IIHF, NHL, NHLPA and Hockey Canada, and invested more than $30 million in capital assets, including two major expansions. He helped secure funding for the D.K. (Doc) Seaman Resource Centre in 2009. Hay retired from The Hall in 2013, and was elected in the Builder Category in 2015.

PAT QUINN *(right)*

Quinn made his NHL debut in 1968-69 with the Toronto Maple Leafs, and also played for Vancouver and the Atlanta Flames, where he was captain, over nine years. After retirement, he held executive, managerial and/or coaching positions with Philadelphia, Los Angeles, Vancouver, Toronto, Edmonton and with Hockey Canada. He was a two-time recipient of the Jack Adams Award as the NHL's Coach of the Year and was head coach of gold-medal-winning Team Canada at the 2002 Olympic Winter Games. Quinn was a member of The Hall's Selection Committee from 1998 to 2013 and assumed the role of chairman of the board in 2013. Although he was chairman for only a short period, his contributions to The Hall's comprehensive selection process overview in 2013-14 were invaluable, as improvements were formulated prior to his untimely passing on November 23, 2014. Quinn was inducted into the Builder Category in 2016.

LANNY MCDONALD *(left)*

McDonald earned his Honoured Member status following an outstanding 16-season career that included the Toronto Maple Leafs, Colorado Rockies and Calgary Flames, and concluded with hoisting the Stanley Cup with Calgary in 1989. Following his playing career, he served as vice-president with the Flames, as well as general manager of Team Canada at the 2001 and 2002 World Championship and director of player personnel for Canada's gold-medal-winning team in 2004. McDonald was inducted into The Hall in the Player Category in 1992. A clever businessman and loved by the hockey world, McDonald joined The Hall's Selection Committee in 2007, serving until he was appointed by the board of directors to succeed Pat Quinn in the role of chairman on July 1, 2015.

JEFF DENOMME *(right)*

Denomme joined The Hall as an intern in 1986. His career would include the role of director, finance and operations, where he was instrumental in the design, development and operational planning for The Hall's $27-million relocation and expansion from the CNE Grounds to BCE (Brookfield) Place in Toronto in 1993. At age 27, he was appointed vice-president, operations and treasurer. Five years later, he assumed the role of president, chief operating officer and treasurer, and in 2013 was appointed president and chief executive officer. Denomme's hands-on management style, together with his contributions in strategic planning, exhibition/facility design, marketing partnerships, information technology and corporate finance, have provided the leadership and vision to support The Hall's economic sustainability and its ongoing growth and development.

ROAD TRIP!

For those who can't make it to downtown Toronto, The Hall has an Outreach Program that brings mobile exhibits and interactive games to communities. Over the years, the popular program has been part of charity events, tournaments and fundraisers of all sorts, and, when combined with The Hall's travelling roadshows, has managed to bring hockey history to fans everywhere.

Notable recent events have included the NHL Centennial Tour during which The Hall travelled to all 31 NHL cities in 2017, a tribute exhibit to Gordie Howe in which 'Mr. Hockey's sons, Mark, Marty and Murray, took part, a First Nations Hockey Display and visits to the NHL All-Star Game.

While on the road, The Hall invites fans to bring along hockey memorabilia, whether artifacts, photos, game-worn jerseys or equipment, for appraisal and possible inclusion into the collection. It's all part of growing the game's legacy — in this case, very much from the grassroots level.

Notwithstanding the great strides it has made over the years, The Hall proactively pursues new opportunities to further advance itself as a cultural institution and popular destination attraction. This includes a newly-established endowment fund in support of capital investments, outreach programs and institutional legacy projects, launched during the dual celebration of The Hall's 75th anniversary and its 25th year in its heritage location.

Among The Hall's goals is the expansion of its global reach. Plans include more storytelling, additional artifacts for its collection and a continued push for latest-generation technologies for its exhibits, especially those that can withstand the rigours of hundreds of thousands of hands-on guests each year. The results speak for themselves: Since opening at Brookfield Place in 1993, The Hall has hosted more than seven million visitors, typically ranging from travelling youth teams to families to couples sporting favoured team jerseys, with a harmony of languages and accents hinting at a diversity of home countries and regions.

Beyond its walls, The Hall continues to expand its outreach in new and exciting ways, including through education — its programs are designed within educational system guidelines for students from primary through to high school and even includes an online course offered in colleges. It also visits hockey communities everywhere with travelling exhibits that feature artifacts from its collection, often in support of charities and fundraisers.

"Our continued growth and development depends to a large degree on partnerships, from within the hockey world and from businesses and individuals who are passionate about the game," explains Denomme. "While the prospects for future development and expansion require well-conceived plans to support The Hall's long-term sustainability, we will always strive to give visitors a great experience and preserve the rich history of our game for generations to come."

That experience includes showcasing the game at all levels, including grassroots amateur hockey, women's hockey, aboriginal hockey, sledge hockey, recreational leagues, the NHL and other professional leagues, as well as international and Olympic hockey — truly 'A Hall for All.'

Somewhere, Captain Sutherland is smiling.

Thanks to a partnership with the International Ice Hockey Federation (IIHF), the largest area within The Hall is dedicated to The World of Hockey, focusing on the game's global footprint and successes.

DOUGLAS WAGNER BENTLEY

Member of the celebrated *Pony Line*, with his two brothers Max and Bill Mosienko, Bentley a for the in medium dozen des Black Hawks an consecutive in 1946. Doug d'une classe d'il y ans exceptions remarquable et two spectaculaire, il a marqué 20 buts ou plus au cours de ses 13 saisons il y finish dans le LNH et a été le champion compteur de la Ligue en 1942-43.

JOHN SHERRATT (BLACK JACK) STEWART

Black Jack was a punishing body checker who earned five All-Star nominations during his 12-year NHL career. After a pair of Stanley Cup victories with Detroit, Stewart joined the Chicago Black Hawks, where he served as team captain from 1950 to 1952.

Joueur dont les mises en échec épuisaient l'adversaire, «Black Jack» a participé à cinq rencontres du Match des étoiles au cours de sa carrière de 12 ans dans la LNH. Après avoir remporté deux fois la Coupe Stanley avec Detroit, Stewart a été échangé aux Black Hawks de Chicago, dont il a été le capitaine de 1950 à 1952.

Player Inductee, 1964

Intronisé à titre de joueur – 1964

Syd Howe played positions as well a year NHL career. A five NHL clubs, he his 12-year stay wi where he played o championship tear a game against the February 3, 1944.

Player Inductee, 1

ANGUS D. CAMPBELL

MARTIN BARRY

ber of

Durant ses étoiles

PORTRAITS IN EXCELLENCE

The 'Great Wall'

ward
uring his 17-
played for
embered for
it Red Wings,
ley Cup
ed six goals in
Rangers on

Syd Howe a évolué aux trois positions d'avant et à la défense au cours de sa carrière de 17 ans dans la LNH. Bien qu'il ait porté l'uniforme de cinq clubs de la LNH, c'est dans celui des Red Wings de Detroit qu'on se souvient le mieux de lui. Il y a joué pendant 12 saisons et y a gagné la Coupe Stanley à trois reprises. Le 3 février 1944, il a marqué six buts contre les Rangers de New York.

Intronisé à titre de joueur – 1965

TOMMY) LOCKHART

It's probably the most visited wall in all of Canada. It's certainly the most compelling in all of hockey.

The portrait wall in the Great Hall features the artist-drawn likeness and biography of every Honoured Member, and, along with all the major NHL trophies displayed nearby, helps make the dramatic room the core sanctuary of the game's history.

Until now, the portraits of hockey's greatest players, builders and referees and linesmen have only been viewed by visitors to The Hall. For the first time in print, they're being presented in their entirety (399 portraits through the 2017 induction year) in this special anniversary book — an elegant way to help celebrate The Hall's 75th year.

19 45

HOBEY BAKER | **P**

SIR MONTAGU ALLAN | **B**

LORD STANLEY OF PRESTON | **B**

FRANK CALDER | **B**

WILLIAM HEWITT | **B**

19 50

SCOTTY DAVIDSON | **P**

19 52

DICKIE BOON | **P**

P = PLAYER
B = BUILDER
R/L = REFEREE/LINESMAN

CHARLIE GARDINER | **P**

EDDIE GERARD | **P**

FRANK MCGEE | **P**

HOWIE MORENZ | **P**

TOMMY PHILLIPS | **P**

HARVEY PULFORD | **P**

HOD STUART | **P**

GEORGES VÉZINA | **P**

19 47

DUBBIE BOWIE | **P**

DIT CLAPPER | **P**

AUREL JOLIAT | **P**

FRANK NIGHBOR | **P**

LESTER PATRICK | **P**

EDDIE SHORE | **P**

CYCLONE TAYLOR | **P**

FRANCIS NELSON | **B**

WILLIAM NORTHEY | **B**

JOHN ROSS ROBERTSON | **B**

CLAUDE ROBINSON | **B**

CAPTAIN JAMES T. SUTHERLAND | **B**

19 49

DAN BAIN | **P**

ART ROSS | **P**

GRAHAM DRINKWATER | **P**

MIKE GRANT | **P**

SI GRIFFIS | **P**

NEWSY LALONDE | **P**

JOE MALONE | **P**

GEORGE RICHARDSON | **P**

HARRY TRIHEY | **P**

FRANK PATRICK | **B**

BILL COOK | **P**

MOOSE GOHEEN | **P**

ERNIE JOHNSON | **P**

MICKEY MACKAY | **P**

NELS STEWART | **P**

19 58

FRANK BOUCHER | **P**

KING CLANCY | **P**

SPRAGUE CLEGHORN | **P**

ALEX CONNELL | **P**

RED DUTTON | **P**

FRANK FOYSTON | **P**

FRANK FREDRICKSON | **P**

HERB GARDINER | **P**

GEORGE HAY | **P**

DICK IRVIN | **P**

SENATOR DONAT
RAYMOND | **B**

CONN SMYTHE | **B**

LLOYD TURNER | **B**

19 59

JACK ADAMS | **P**

CY DENNENY | **P**

TINY THOMPSON | **P**

19 60

CHARLIE CONACHER | **P**

HAP DAY | **P**

GEORGE HAINSWORTH | **P**

JOE HALL | **P**

PERCY LESUEUR | **P**

FRANK RANKIN | **P**

MAURICE RICHARD | **P**

MILT SCHMIDT | **P**

19 62

PUNCH BROADBENT | **P**

HARRY HYLAND | **P**

STEAMER MAXWELL | **P**

REG NOBLE | **P**

SWEENEY SCHRINER | **P**

ALF SMITH | **P**

FRANK AHEARN | **B**

RUSTY CRAWFORD | **P**

JACK DARRAGH | **P**

JIMMY GARDNER | **P**

BILLY GILMOUR | **P**

EBBIE GOODFELLOW | **P**

SHORTY GREEN | **P**

RILEY HERN | **P**

TOM HOOPER | **P**

 CHING JOHNSON | **P**

DUKE KEATS | **P**

HUGH LEHMAN | **P**

GEORGE MCNAMARA | **P**

PADDY MORAN | **P**

GEORGE DUDLEY | **B**

JAMES NORRIS | **B**

AL PICKARD | **B**

 BUCK BOUCHER | **P**

 SYLVIO MANTHA | **P**

 JACK WALKER | **P**

 CHARLES ADAMS | **B**

 GENERAL JOHN REED KILPATRICK | **B**

 FRANK SELKE | **B**

19 61

 SYL APPS | **P**

 OLIVER SEIBERT | **P**

 BRUCE STUART | **P**

 GEORGE BROWN | **B**

 PAUL LOICQ | **B**

 FRED WAGHORNE | **B**

 CHAUCER ELLIOTT | **R/L**

 MICKEY ION | **R/L**

 COOPER SMEATON | **R/L**

 WALTER BROWN | **B**

 FRED HUME | **B**

 JAMES NORRIS | **B**

 AMBROSE O'BRIEN | **B**

 FRANK SMITH | **B**

 MIKE RODDEN | **R/L**

19 63

 HARRY CAMERON | **P**

BOUSE HUTTON | **P**

JACK LAVIOLETTE | **P**

BILLY MCGIMSIE | **P**

DIDIER PITRE | **P**

JOE PRIMEAU | **P**

JACK RUTTAN | **P**

EARL SEIBERT | **P**

BULLET JOE SIMPSON | **P**

While each newly-elected Honoured Member of The Hall reacts to induction in a different way, pride, respect and emotion seem to be common threads that connect their feelings. Here are a few memorable quotes from the game's greats over the years as they reflected on what it means to receive hockey's highest honour.

The awards I won were for one season's play or a month's work in the playoffs. To be named to the Hall of Fame is to be recognized for what you did in your lifetime, and that's the best reward of all.

JACQUES PLANTE | CLASS OF 1978

When I got the call, I had chills going up and down my spine when I realized the honour and privilege.

JOEY MULLEN | CLASS OF 2000

Having my hobby and love for a sport become my livelihood really allowed me to live out my dream.

MATS SUNDIN | CLASS OF 2012

At 17, Larry Robinson, Denis Potvin and Raymond Bourque were planning to go to the NHL. At 17, I was planning to go to the beach. As it turned out, my game plan in hockey was the same one we had surfing 30 years in San Diego. I caught the big wave and rode it as hard as I could for as long as I could.

CHRIS CHELIOS | CLASS OF 2013

As a player, this is something I have worked for all of my life.

VIACHESLAV FETISOV | CLASS OF 2001

Joining Borje Salming and Mats Sundin in the Hall of Fame as the third Swedish member makes it especially gratifying for me.

PETER FORSBERG | CLASS OF 2014

To be a member of the Hall of Fame is one of the best honours after you retire. It means you made it. It means you gave something to hockey after all those years.

YVAN COURNOYER | CLASS OF 1982

SOME HONOURED

Just to be the fifth (female inductee) is pretty amazing. What's amazing is that we're finally in the Hockey Hall of Fame. This the best thing that can happen to women's hockey.

DANIELLE GOYETTE | CLASS OF 2017

Making the Hall of Fame was the biggest hockey thrill. I'm proud of that. I gave everything I had to the game and it gave me everything.

PIERRE PILOTE | CLASS OF 1975

I was stunned! It is the single greatest honour of my life.

BRIAN KILREA | CLASS OF 2003

Going back into the 1920s and maybe even into the teens, there has been one heck of a lot of great hockey players who have played this game who are in the Hall of Fame, but there are a lot who didn't make it, so I feel very honoured to have been voted in.

TED LINDSAY | CLASS OF 1966

I will never forget the day Pat Quinn called to say that I was being inducted into the Hockey Hall of Fame. It's an honour to be the third woman to be inducted and to be recognized with my hockey heroes I grew up watching.

GERALDINE HEANEY | CLASS OF 2013

Next to winning the Stanley Cup, my greatest thrill in the game came in 1976 when I was inducted into the Hockey Hall of Fame. What an honour that was. I couldn't believe it! In fact, I broke down.

JOHNNY BOWER | CLASS OF 1976

It is the highest honour and achievement a player can receive when inducted with the greatest hockey players of all time.

DARRYL SITTLER | CLASS OF 1989

MEMORIES

BARNEY STANLEY | **P**

MARTY WALSH | **P**

HARRY WATSON | **P**

HARRY WESTWICK | **P**

FRED WHITCROFT | **P**

PHAT WILSON | **P**

LEO DANDURAND | **B**

TOMMY GORMAN | **B**

FRANK DILIO | **B**

BILL CHADWICK | **R/L**

19 65

MARTY BARRY | **P**

CLINT BENEDICT | **P**

ART FARRELL | **P**

RED HORNER | **P**

SYD HOWE | **P**

MAX BENTLEY | **P**

TOE BLAKE | **P**

BUTCH BOUCHARD | **P**

FRANK BRIMSEK | **P**

TED KENNEDY | **P**

ELMER LACH | **P**

TED LINDSAY | **P**

BABE PRATT | **P**

BILL COWLEY | **P**

JIMMY DUNN | **B**

JIM HENDY | **B**

19 69

SID ABEL | **P**

BRYAN HEXTALL | **P**

RED KELLY | **P**

ROY WORTERS | **P**

BUSHER JACKSON | **P**

GORDON ROBERTS | **P**

TERRY SAWCHUK | **P**

COONEY WEILAND | **P**

ARTHUR WIRTZ | **B**

19 72

JEAN BÉLIVEAU | **P**

BERNIE GEOFFRION | **P**

MAJOR FRED
MCLAUGHLIN | **B**

BOBBY HEWITSON | **R/L**

19 64

DOUG BENTLEY | **P**

BILL DURNAN | **P**

BABE SIEBERT | **P**

BLACK JACK STEWART | **P**

ANGUS CAMPBELL | **B**

JACK MARSHALL | **P**

BILL MOSIENKO | **P**

BLAIR RUSSEL | **P**

ERNIE RUSSELL | **P**

FRED SCANLAN | **P**

FOSTER HEWITT | **B**

TOM LOCKHART | **B**

19 66

KEN REARDON | **P**

CLARENCE CAMPBELL | **B**

19 67

TURK BRODA | **P**

NEIL COLVILLE | **P**

HARRY OLIVER | **P**

RED STOREY | **R/L**

19 68

AL LEADER | **B**

BRUCE NORRIS | **B**

19 70

BABE DYE | **P**

BILL GADSBY | **P**

TOM JOHNSON | **P**

BOB LEBEL | **B**

19 71

HAP HOLMES | **P**

GORDIE HOWE | **P**

HOOLEY SMITH | **P**

WESTON ADAMS | **B**

19 73

DOUG HARVEY | **P**

CHARLIE RAYNER | **P**

TOMMY SMITH | **P**

HON. HARTLAND
MOLSON | **B**

FRANK UDVARI | **R/L**

1974

BILLY BURCH | **P**

ART COULTER | **P**

TOMMY DUNDERDALE | **P**

DICKIE MOORE | **P**

CHARLES HAY | **B**

PIERRE PILOTE | **P**

FRANK BUCKLAND | **B**

WILLIAM JENNINGS | **B**

1976

JOHNNY BOWER | **P**

BILL QUACKENBUSH | **P**

JACK GIBSON | **B**

P.D. ROSS | **B**

ANDY BATHGATE | **P**

JACQUES PLANTE | **P**

MARCEL PRONOVOST | **P**

J.P. BICKELL | **B**

SAM POLLOCK | **B**

THAYER TUTT | **B**

1979

HARRY HOWELL | **P**

1981

JOHNNY BUCYK | **P**

FRANK MAHOVLICH | **P**

ALLAN STANLEY | **P**

JOHN ASHLEY | **R/L**

1982

YVAN COURNOYER | **P**

ROD GILBERT | **P**

PHIL ESPOSITO | **P**

JACQUES LEMAIRE | **P**

BERNIE PARENT | **P**

PUNCH IMLACH | **B**

JAKE MILFORD | **B**

1985

GERRY CHEEVERS | **P**

BERT OLMSTEAD | **P**

TOMMY IVAN | **B**

ANATOLI TARASOV | **B**

CARL VOSS | **B**

1975

GEORGE ARMSTRONG | **P**

ACE BAILEY | **P**

GORDIE DRILLON | **P**

GLENN HALL | **P**

WILLIAM WIRTZ | **B**

1977

ALEX DELVECCHIO | **P**

TIM HORTON | **P**

BUNNY AHEARNE | **B**

HAROLD BALLARD | **B**

JOE CATTARINICH | **B**

1978

BOBBY ORR | **P**

HENRI RICHARD | **P**

GORDON JUCKES | **B**

1980

HARRY LUMLEY | **P**

LYNN PATRICK | **P**

GUMP WORSLEY | **P**

JACK BUTTERFIELD | **B**

NORM ULLMAN | **P**

EMILE FRANCIS | **B**

1983

KEN DRYDEN | **P**

BOBBY HULL | **P**

STAN MIKITA | **P**

HARRY SINDEN | **B**

1984

JEAN RATELLE | **P**

JOHN MARIUCCI | **B**

RUDY PILOUS | **B**

1986

LEO BOIVIN | **P**

DAVE KEON | **P**

SERGE SAVARD | **P**

BILL HANLEY | **B**

THE HALL SELECTION

On April 27, 1958, for the first time, a Selection Committee was formed to elect Honoured Members to be inducted into the Hockey Hall of Fame. Prior to that date, the board of directors had handled all affairs pertaining to The Hall, including the election of Honoured Members.

The following list includes all those who have participated in the election of the greatest players, builders and officials to have served the game.

Keith Allen | September 1996-September 1997

Kevin Allen | September 1994-September 1998

Al Arbour | June 2001-June 2006

Jean Béliveau | June 1981-September 1995

Scotty Bowman | June 2003-June 2017

David Branch | June 2009-present

Walter Brown | September 1960-June 1964

Brian Burke | June 2012-present

Walter Bush | September 1994-September 1995

Colin Campbell | June 2005-present

Ed Chynoweth | June 1991-June 2007

Bob Clarke | June 2014-present

Charles Coleman | June 1972-June 1984

Neil Colville | June 1977-June 1983

Murray Costello | September 1994-September 1995

John Davidson | April 1999-present

Marc DeFoy | June 2012-present

Alex Delvecchio | June 1985-June 1993

Marcel Desjardins | April 1958-June 1980

George Dudley | April 1958-September 1959

Eric Duhatschek | June 2004-present

Jimmy Dunnell | June 1961-June 1976

Milt Dunnell | April 1958-June 1991

Red Dutton | April 1958-June 1976

Jan-Ake Edvinsson | June 2006-June 2011

Mike Emrick | June 2001-June 2015

Michael Farber | June 2007-present

Stan Fischler | September 1994-September 1995

Red Fisher | June 1985-June 2003

Tom Fitzgerald | June 1973-June 1983

Cliff Fletcher | September 1994-June 2002

Emile Francis | June 1990-June 2008

Ron Francis | June 2016-present

Danny Gallivan | April 1958-June 1992

Mike Gartner | June 2009-present

Ebbie Goodfellow | June 1966-June 1984

Jim Gregory | June 1993-July 2013

George Gross | June 1992-September 1998

Bill Hay | June 1980-September 1997

Anders Hedberg | June 2012-present

Bobby Hewitson | April 1958-June 1967

Dick Irvin | September 1996-June 2010

COMMITTEE MEMBERS

Tommy Ivan | June 1980-September 1995

Gordon Juckes | June 1965-June 1989

Jari Kurri | June 2016-present

Igor Larionov | June 2011-present

John Mariucci | June 1977-June 1985

Frank Mathers | September 1994-September 1996

Lanny McDonald | June 2007-June 2015

Pierre McGuire | June 2018-present

Bob McKenzie | June 2016-present

Gerry Meehan | September 1994-September 1995

Stan Mikita | September 1997-June 2005

Tim Moriarty | June 1977-June 1993

Scotty Morrison | June 1989-September 1997

Lou Nanne | September 1994-September 1995

James Norris | June 1965-June 1965

Baz O'Meara | April 1958-June 1971

Bobby Orr | September 1998-June 2000

Dick Patrick | September 1994-June 2006

Lynn Patrick | June 1977-June 1979

Lester Patrick | April 1958-September 1959

Marty Pavelich | June 1992-June 2006

Yvon Pedneault | June 2005-June 2011

Jean Perron | September 1994-September 1995

Al Pickard | April 1958-June 1964

Bud Poile | June 1984-June 1993

David Poile | June 2014-present

Jim Proudfoot | September 1994-June 2000

Pat Quinn | September 1998-July 2013

Bertrand Raymond | September 1994-June 2004

Lefty Reid | June 1968-June 1988

Luc Robitaille | June 2014-present

Fran Rosa | June 1984-September 1995

Glen Sather | September 1994-September 1995

Serge Savard | September 1994-July 2013

Frank Selke Sr. | September 1960-June 1979

Frank Selke Jr. | June 1991-June 2006

Harry Sinden | September 1994-June 2011

Peter Stastny | June 2007-June 2015

Al Strachan | June 1993-September 1995

Cyclone Taylor | September 1960-June 1979

Bill Torrey | June 2007-May 2018

Frank Udvari | September 1994-June 2004

Bill Wirtz | September 1994-September 1995

19 87

BOBBY CLARKE | **P**

ED GIACOMIN | **P**

JACQUES LAPERRIÈRE | **P**

JOHN ZIEGLER | **B**

MATT PAVELICH | **R/L**

19 88

TONY ESPOSITO | **P**

VLADISLAV TRETIAK | **P**

FATHER DAVID BAUER | **B**

19 90

BILL BARBER | **P**

FERN FLAMAN | **P**

GILBERT PERREAULT | **P**

BUD POILE | **B**

19 91

WOODY DUMART | **P**

BOB GAINEY | **P**

LANNY MCDONALD | **P**

KEITH ALLEN | **B**

BOB JOHNSON | **B**

FRANK MATHERS | **B**

19 93

GUY LAPOINTE | **P**

LIONEL CONACHER | **P**

HARRY WATSON | **P**

BRIAN O'NEILL | **B**

19 95

BUN COOK | **P**

LARRY ROBINSON | **P**

GUNTHER SABETZKI | **B**

BILL TORREY | **B**

19 98

ROY CONACHER | **P**

MICHEL GOULET | **P**

PETER STASTNY | **P**

PERE ATHOL MURRAY | **B**

19 99

WAYNE GRETZKY | **P**

SCOTTY MORRISON | **B**

GUY LAFLEUR | **P**

BUDDY O'CONNOR | **P**

BRAD PARK | **P**

ED SNIDER | **B**

GEORGE HAYES | **R/L**

19 89

HERBIE LEWIS | **P**

DARRYL SITTLER | **P**

MIKE BOSSY | **P**

DENIS POTVIN | **P**

BOB PULFORD | **P**

CLINT SMITH | **P**

SCOTTY BOWMAN | **B**

NEIL ARMSTRONG | **R/L**

19 92

MARCEL DIONNE | **P**

EDGAR LAPRADE | **P**

STEVE SHUTT | **P**

BILLY SMITH | **P**

FRANK GRIFFITHS | **B**

SEYMOUR KNOX III | **B**

FRED PAGE | **B**

JOHN D'AMICO | **R/L**

19 94

19 96

BOBBY BAUER | **P**

BORJE SALMING | **P**

AL ARBOUR | **B**

19 97

MARIO LEMIEUX | **P**

BRYAN TROTTIER | **P**

GLEN SATHER | **B**

ANDY VAN
HELLEMOND | **R/L**

20 00

JOEY MULLEN | **P**

DENIS SAVARD | **P**

WALTER BUSH | **B**

20 01

VIACHESLAV FETISOV | **P**

MIKE GARTNER | **P**

DALE HAWERCHUK | **P**

JARI KURRI | **P**

CRAIG PATRICK | **B**

20 02

BERNIE FEDERKO | **P**

CLARK GILLIES | **P**

ROD LANGWAY | **P**

ROGER NEILSON | **B**

LARRY MURPHY | **P**

CLIFF FLETCHER | **B**

20 05

VALERI KHARLAMOV | **P**

CAM NEELY | **P**

MURRAY COSTELLO | **B**

20 06

DICK DUFF | **P**

JIM GREGORY | **B**

20 08

GLENN ANDERSON | **P**

IGOR LARIONOV | **P**

ED CHYNOWETH | **B**

RAY SCAPINELLO | **R/L**

20 09

BRETT HULL | **P**

JIMMY DEVELLANO | **B**

DOC SEAMAN | **B**

20 11

ED BELFOUR | **P**

DOUG GILMOUR | **P**

MARK HOWE | **P**

JOE NIEUWENDYK | **P**

20 12

BRENDAN SHANAHAN | **P**

FRED SHERO | **B**

20 14

ROB BLAKE | **P**

PETER FORSBERG | **P**

DOMINIK HASEK | **P**

MIKE MODANO | **P**

PAT BURNS | **B**

**20 03**

 GRANT FUHR | **P**

 PAT LAFONTAINE | **P**

 BRIAN KILREA | **B**

 MIKE ILITCH | **B**

**20 04**

 RAY BOURQUE | **P**

PAUL COFFEY | **P**

 PATRICK ROY | **P**

 HERB BROOKS | **B**

 HARLEY HOTCHKISS | **B**

**20 07**

 RON FRANCIS | **P**

 AL MACINNIS | **P**

 MARK MESSIER | **P**

 SCOTT STEVENS | **P**

 BRIAN LEETCH | **P**

 LUC ROBITAILLE | **P**

 STEVE YZERMAN | **P**

 LOU LAMORIELLO | **B**

**20 10**

 DINO CICCARELLI | **P**

 CAMMI GRANATO | **P**

 ANGELA JAMES | **P**

 PAVEL BURE | **P**

 ADAM OATES | **P**

 JOE SAKIC | **P**

 MATS SUNDIN | **P**

**20 13**

 CHRIS CHELIOS | **P**

 GERALDINE HEANEY | **P**

 SCOTT NIEDERMAYER | **P**

 BILL McCREARY | **R/L**

**20 15**

 SERGEI FEDOROV | **P**

 PHIL HOUSLEY | **P**

 NICKLAS LIDSTROM | **P**

 CHRIS PRONGER | **P**

 ANGELA RUGGIERO | **P**

 BILL HAY | **B**

PETER
KARMANOS JR. | **B**

ERIC LINDROS | **P**

SERGEI MAKAROV | **P**

ROGIE VACHON | **P**

PAT QUINN | **B**

DAVE ANDREYCHUK | **P**

DANIELLE GOYETTE | **P**

PAUL KARIYA | **P**

MARK RECCHI | **P**

TEEMU SELANNE | **P**

CLARE DRAKE | **B**

JEREMY JACOBS | **B**

HE PORTRAIT ARTISTS

Amidst the lustre of the Great Hall, alongside the magnificent Stanley Cup and overlooking the NHL's merit trophies, are the portraits the Honoured Members, majestically displayed on plaques and enjoyed by legions of visitors to The Hall each year.

"I love faces," Irma Coucill once said, the original artist responsible for the portraits.

Born in London, Ontario in 1918, Coucill came to be the official artist of The Hall through happenstance. One day in 1957, her husband, Walter, was enjoying lunch at the Arts and Letters Club in Toronto when he overheard someone mention that The Hall was looking for an artist. He excused himself and mentioned that his wife was just what they were looking for. Coucill was given the job.

Her first task was herculean: She was given photographs of 60 Honoured Members and asked to draw portraits of each. Setting up an illustration board, she went about her work and delivered 60 impeccable portraits, one per day, for which she was paid $35 each.

The Hall proudly unveiled Coucill's portraits at the 1958 induction luncheon at the CNE to an incredible reception. Trouble was, Coucill was not invited to the male-only affair; her husband was there in her place. In 1972, The Hall changed its policy and women were finally included in the ceremonies. Before his induction speech that year, Bernie Geoffrion looked over at Coucill and said, "It's nice to see a lady here. I'm tired of seeing all your ugly mugs!" 'Boom Boom' received an extended round of applause.

Coucill altered her style over the years and felt that her portraits were getting stronger. She approached The Hall and asked if she could re-do her earliest portraits at "No charge." She completed her final portrait for The Hall in 2012 at age 94. It was of Mats Sundin, the last of 370 portraits she contributed to The Hall's history. She passed away on November 29, 2015.

Ironically, Coucill's successor was inspired by her work. After visiting The Hall at the CNE as a child, Paul Riley was captivated by the portraits of the hockey legends. "I saw Irma's work on the walls (of The Hall) and it floored me."

Riley has worked in the animation industry since 1984. Just like Coucill, he was given a serendipitous opportunity to produce The Hall portraits. He was coaching his daughter's hockey team with Craig Campbell, Manager of Resource Centre and Archives for The Hall, who also had a daughter on the team. Riley mentioned that he'd love to create the portraits, and Campbell said that The Hall was looking. Riley submitted his portfolio, and the committee found his style remarkably similar to that of Coucill. He got the job. His first portraits were of the Class of 2013: Chris Chelios, Geraldine Heaney, Scott Niedermayer, Brendan Shanahan and Fred Shero.

"It was something I'd always wished I could do," he told the *Newmarket Era*. "I've drawn since I can remember, so this has gone hand-in-hand, and to me (is) why the Hockey Hall of Fame is the coolest job I could have. It was a dream come true and I have to pinch myself."

CREDITS

BIBLIOGRAPHY

Brown, William. *Doug: The Doug Harvey Story*
Montreal, Quebec: Vehicule Press, 2002

Conway, Russ. *Game Misconduct: Alan Eagleson and the Corruption of Hockey*
Toronto, Ontario: MacFarlane, Walter & Ross, 1997

Fitsell, J. William. *Captain James T. Sutherland: The Grand Old Man of Hockey. The Battle for the Original Hockey Hall of Fame*
Kingston, Ontario: Quarry Press, 2014

Fitsell, J. William. *Hockey's Captains, Colonels and Kings*
Erin, Ontario: Boston Mills Publishing, 1989

Griffith, Jeffrey. *Commemorating Greatness: the Hockey Hall of Fame's Celebration of Hockey, Canada and the Individual*
Thesis: California State University, Fullerton, 2013

McParland, Kelly. *The Lives of Conn Smythe*
Bolton, Ontario: Fenn Publishing, 2011

Oliver, Greg. *Blue Lines, Goal Lines & Bottom Lines*
Toronto, Ontario: ECW Press, 2016

O'Reilly, Terry. *This I Know: Marketing Lessons from Under the Influence*
Toronto, Ontario: Penguin Random House Canada, 2017

Orr, Bobby. *Orr: My Story*
Toronto, Ontario: Penguin Canada Books Inc., 2013

Podnieks, Andrew. *Hockey Hall of Fame: Honoured Members*
Bolton, Ontario: Fenn Publishing, 2003

Reid, Maurice 'Lefty'. *I Remember: Recollections of Former Hockey Hall of Fame Curator and Director, 1968-1992*
Self-published: 2015

Selke, Frank J. *Behind the Cheering*
Toronto, Ontario: McClelland and Stewart Ltd., 1962

Stein, Gil. *Power Play: An Inside Look at the Big Business of the National Hockey League*
Land O' Lakes, Florida: Birch Lane Press, 1997

Zweig, Eric. *Art Ross: The Hockey Legend Who Built The Bruins*
Toronto, Ontario: Dundurn Press, 2015

AUTHOR'S ACKNOWLEDGMENTS

To research and write the definitive and very entertaining history of the Hockey Hall of Fame has been one of the most interesting and rewarding projects I've ever been entrusted to create.

My very sincere thanks go to the staff of the Hockey Hall of Fame. **Jeff Denomme**, the Hockey Hall of Fame's president & CEO, was generous with his time and guidance. **Peter Jagla**, vice-president of marketing and attraction services, was an enthusiastic supporter, providing thoughtful analysis and suggestions. **Phil Pritchard**, vice-president of the Resource Centre and curator, contributed great ideas and content. Huge thanks, also, to **Craig Campbell** and **Steve Poirier** for finding the perfect photos to accompany the history, **Kelly Masse** for proving memories of Induction Weekends, as well as **Ron Ellis**, **Jackie Schwartz** and the rest of the staff.

Former chairman **Scotty Morrison** and **Lefty Reid**, who served as curator, provided important content for the book. Former Hockey Hall of Fame president **David Taylor** as well as the former marketing team of **Bryan Black** and **Christine Simpson**, added welcomed memories from their years at The Hall.

Bill Fitsell's immense knowledge of Kingston's hockey history, as well as his books, *Captain James T. Sutherland: The Grand Old Man of Hockey. The Battle for the Original Hockey Hall of Fame and Hockey's Captains, Colonels and Kings* were extremely beneficial.

Two other publications were of great help to researching The Hall: Jeffrey Griffith's 2013 thesis from California State University, Fullerton, titled *Commemorating Greatness: the Hockey Hall of Fame's Celebration of Hockey, Canada and the Individual* as well as Maurice 'Lefty' Reid's self-published *I Remember: Recollections of Former Hockey Hall of Fame Curator and Director, 1968-1992*.

Shannon Mooney, Associate Archivist, Corporate Archives at BMO Financial Group, was most generous in sharing information and photographs regarding the Bank of Montreal's history in downtown Toronto.

Terry O'Reilly, **Darren Clarke**, **L. Harvey Gold**, **David Huband** and **Rick Wharton** provided terrific information on the creation of The Hall's award-winning TV commercials.

The Hockey Hall of Fame's incredible Resource Centre provided much of the research for 'The Hall,' supplemented by the archives of the *Toronto (Daily) Star* and *Globe and Mail*.

The publisher, Griffintown Media showed great vision, creativity and patience in creating this wonderful history of the Hockey Hall of Fame on its special 75/25 anniversary. Thank you **Jim McRae**, **Katrysha Gellis**, **Salma Belhaffaf** and **Jim Hynes**.

On a personal note, I lost my mother, **Margaret England**, during the creation of this book. She was my most enthusiastic supporter in every venture in which I've been involved, and I miss her dearly. I would also like to thank **Nancy Niklas**, **Dale Shea**, **Tim Burgess**, **Andrea Orlick**, **Kim Cooke**, **Steve Waxman**, **Gerry England**, **Hersh Borenstein** and **Paul Patskou** for their support and friendship.

And to those, like me, who have lost full days wandering through the Hockey Hall of Fame, embracing the Stanley Cup, examining every artifact, reading every caption (and yes, playing every game), I thank you for providing the inspiration behind 'The Hall.'